The Folklore of Birds

THE FOLKLORE OF BIRDS

by

Laura C. Martin

Illustrations by Mauro Magellan

The Globe Pequot Press

Old Saybrook, Connecticut

Cover and text illustrations by Mauro Magellan
Book design by Nancy Freeborn

Library of Congress Cataloging-in-Publication Data

Martin, Laura C.
  The folklore of birds / by Laura C. Martin. — 1st ed.
     p. cm.
   ISBN 1-56440-216-9
   ISBN 1-56440-872-8 (paperback)
   1. Birds—Folklore. 2. Birds—United States—Folklore.
I. Title.
GR735.M37 1993
398.24'528—dc20   92-39582

Folklore of Birds

Manufactured in the United States of America
First Edition/Fifth Printing

To my son, David Sheffield Martin, Jr.

ACKNOWLEDGMENTS

Many thanks to Laura Strom at Globe Pequot Press and
to my friend and agent, Sally McMillan.
Special thanks go to my favorite bird lady, Micky Bidwell,
for her interest, enthusiasm, and technical knowledge.

CONTENTS

INTRODUCTION

Bird watchers, or "birders" as they like to call themselves, enjoy their hobby with a fervor that surpasses interest and borders on passion. A true birder will think nothing of hopping in the car and driving hundreds of miles on the chance of catching sight of an unusual or rare winged creature.

Although today's birder is armed with the best lenses and cameras that technology can supply and man can buy, the art of and passion for watching birds is ageless.

Primitive cultures considered birds magical creatures. Unlike humans and other beasts, birds were not earthbound but could soar through the heavens. Many cultures even worshiped birds and believed that they could bring rain, predict the future, and bring good or ill luck.

Today's birds fill every environmental niche imaginable, from the ocean to the desert, the canyons to the mountaintops. The diversity of birds is staggering, their beauty unimaginable until you see it with your own eyes. Because of their beauty and their ability to fly, many stories and legends have been written about birds, and many superstitions and folktales surround them. No words, however, can adequately describe the grace and beauty that these winged creatures offer; no book or song or poem can express the sheer exhilaration of seeing the splendor of a bird in flight.

The Folklore of Birds is a celebration of the beauty and glory of the birds, their histories and personalities, and their influence on the world of man. The birds discussed in this volume represent only a fraction of the birds found throughout the world. The ones chosen for this book are all found in the United States, although the associated folklore may span the continents. For example, although the American blackbird is distinctly different from the European species, many of the stores and legends refer to the "blackbirds" as a group without differentiating between genus and species.

Sadly, today it is estimated that more than 1,000 species of birds have suffered extinction. In exploring the nature and wonder of birds, and in becoming more intimately familiar with them, it is my hope that we will develop a sensitivity and a renewed appreciation for these fellow creatures.

The song of the bird is the song of hope, a fervent prayer that man will learn to live in harmony with all inhabitants of the earth. Centuries from now, when the world of man has changed and we are perhaps still struggling to communicate with one another, the voice of the bird will still sing true, a universal language uniting us in a common song.

BLACK-FOOTED ALBATROSS

COMMON NAME: Albatross, Black-footed
SCIENTIFIC NAME: *Diomedea nigripes*

DESCRIPTION: Albatrosses are character-ized by their tremendous wingspread. The black-footed albatross, with a length of 28 inches, has a wingspread of 80 inches. This is the only dark albatross found near the United States. It has a dark, heavy, hooked bill with a whitish mark on the face encircling the bill. Upper tail coverts have a narrow white band. As the common name indicates, the feet of this bird are dark, and the front three toes are webbed. The albatross is similar to, but much larger than, the petrel. The plumage of the immature albatross is distinctly different from that of the adult.

HABITAT AND RANGE: The albatross is rarely seen near shore but soars over the Pacif-ic Ocean from the Bering Sea to Baja California. Nests are found on deserted islands and remote shore areas.

A bove the sea, the albatross soars endless-ly, resting only on the wind currents that keep it aloft. When it spots a ship, the bird may make lazy circles around it for days. Albatrosses will occasionally land on the water. Their landings leave a bit to be desired, for the albatross appears to be one of the clumsiest of all creatures. After spending as long as two or three months aloft, they will fall toward the earth and land in an awkward, graceless meet-ing of feathers and water. Unperturbed, these big birds merely shake the water off and right themselves. It was this comical landing that may have earned the birds the nickname, "gooneybird." The Dutch have a similar name, mollyhawk, which means "stupid gull."

In spite of the superstition that it is bad luck to kill an albatross, natives of many oceanic islands regularly ate meat from these birds, as did whalers and sealers visiting the islands. The feathers of several species became commercially important, and millions of birds were killed for their plumage, resulting in the extermination of many colonies and the severe reduction of many more.

It was Samuel Taylor Coleridge who brought the most fame to the albatross with his poem "The Rime of the Ancient Mariner." The sailor in this poem killed an albatross that hovered near the ship, thus breaking a revered cycle of life at sea. He sub-sequently felt great torment and a heaviness of spirit. Today to speak of an albatross around one's neck indicates a heavy and unwieldy problem.

The albatross was thought to bring storms

and high gales and generally bad weather. An ancient superstition suggests that the albatross lays its eggs in a floating nest. It was further believed that these birds were not content to stay with their eggs but would return to lofty heights and even sleep on the wing.

An old poem called "Lalla Rookh" describes it this way:

A ruined temple tower'd so high
That oft the sleeping albatross
Struck the wild ruins with her wing

The name albatross is from the Portugese word *alcatrus,* meaning "bucket or trough on a water wheel," and refers to the bird using its mouth as a pouch or bucket. The genus name *Diomedea* is from the Greek Diomedes, a hero of the Trojan war, whose companions were transformed into birds. The species name *nigripes* is from the Latin words *niger,* meaning "black," and *pes,* meaning "foot."

These birds generally breed on flat, open parts of oceanic islands and feed on squid, surface fish, crustaceans, and whale carcasses.

Each year a single, large egg is laid, and both the male and female care for the egg during an incubation period that may last over two months. It takes approximately ten to twelve years for the albatross to attain breeding maturity.

COMMON NAME: Anhinga
SCIENTIFIC NAME: *Anhinga anhinga*

DESCRIPTION: The male is generally a glossy black color with a greenish iridescent cast. The upper part of the wings are a silver-gray. The female has a grayish brown head, slender neck and breast, and a dark belly. The feet are webbed and end in long, sharp claws that allow the birds to climb easily. A serrated bill helps these birds easily catch fish, which they toss into the air and then gulp down head first.

HABITAT AND RANGE: Anhingas are freshwater birds and can be found in swamps and ponds, particularly in those with abundant vegetation. These birds live along the coasts, from North Carolina to Texas and up the Mississippi Valley north to Arkansas.

ANHINGA

Anhingas are also sometimes called snake-birds because of their habit of swimming with only their long, slender neck protruding out of the water, looking very much like a swimming snake. After emerging from the water, the birds often spread their wings in the sun and sit for a while to dry out their feathers. Another common name is water turkey.

Their nests are awkward and bulky, made of sticks, Spanish moss, and leaves. The genus name *anhinga* is thought to have originated with the Tupi Indians of Brazil, though it has also been suggested that the name may be from the Latin word *anguina,* meaning "snakelike."

This bird's flight usually consists of alternate flapping and sailing, a characteristic that makes the anhinga easy to identify even from a distance. With its long neck, wings, and tail, it looks like a flying cross. When frightened off a perch, these birds sometimes drop like an arrow into the water, and when they surface, only their slender, snakelike neck protrudes above water. When hunting prey, anhingas usually do not plunge but dive from the surface and swim under water.

Anhingas are usually quiet birds, though they sometimes make a low grunting noise. Other than to nest, anhingas spend almost their entire life over or on the water. They are able to drink water straight from the ocean, having well-developed glands that separate out and excrete the dissolved salts from the seawater.

Anhingas are gregarious birds, often forming colonies with herons and ibis.

COMMON NAME: **Bittern, American**

SCIENTIFIC NAME: *Botaurus lentiginosus*

DESCRIPTION: The American bittern measures 24 to 35 inches in length. It is a dark brown bird with lighter yellowish brown streaks on the inner wings and body. The neck has a black stripe and the tips of the wings appear dark when the bird is in flight.

HABITAT AND RANGE: Bitterns are found in marshy areas, both freshwater and brackish, in most areas of the country.

Roasted bittern was once quite a delicacy in England. Today in the British Isles, local populations of this bird are greatly reduced because of its historic desirability. Beryl Rowland wrote in her book *Birds with Human Souls* that in 1802 a single bird cost a

AMERICAN BITTERN

half-guinea, which was about half a week's wages for the average laborer.

A bittern has a rather secretive, solitary lifestyle. When danger approaches, it prefers to protect itself by remaining motionless in tall marsh grass rather than flushing, like other members of this family. To further enhance the masterful camouflage, the bittern points its bill upward and sways from side to side to resemble the moving marsh grass in which it is hiding. If, however, the bird is finally flushed, it will emit a low barking call as it flies off.

This sound is so startling that many legends and folktales have developed to explain it. One story tells of how the bittern pierces a reed with its beak and then blows through it to make its call.

Oliver Goldsmith wrote: "It is impossible for words to give those who have not heard this evening call an adequate idea of its solemnity. It is like the interrupted bellowing of a bull, but hollower, and louder, and is heard at a mile's distance, as if issuing from some formidable being that resided at the bottom of the waters."

The sound created by the bittern caused it to be taken as a symbol of doom and desolation. In the Bible it was prophesied (in Isaiah and Zephaniah) that Babylon and Nineveh were to become a wasteland with the bittern's cry echoing in the ruins of their palaces.

During the Middle Ages, the bittern was considered a symbol of greed, and at one time the bird was even thought to have two stomachs. Renaissance symbolism connected the bittern with idleness, as was indicated by the sixteenth-century proverb "A bittern will never make a good hawk."

Henry David Thoreau called the bittern the "genius of the bog," suggesting that the bird had other, redeeming qualities. The bittern is also called stake driver, because at great distances only one syllable of the bird's song is detectable, a sound resembling the report of a stake being driven. Other common names include thunder pump, dunk-a-doo, and Indian hen.

The genus name is from the Latin word *boatumtauri*, meaning the "bellowing of a bull." This, of course, refers to the great call of the bird. The species name, *lentiginosus*, is from the Latin word *lentigo*, meaning "freckle," and refers to the speckled brown and white plumage of the bird.

The bittern's eyes are placed so that it can see forward when it "freezes" with bill pointed upward to blend in with the reeds of its marsh environment. This gave rise to the common name, sun-gazer. When its bill is in its normal position, pointed forward, a bittern can see food items directly below.

It was at one time believed that the American bittern could actually project light from its breast. This light, which was thought to be as strong as from a lantern, was believed to help the bittern find its prey at night.

COMMON NAME: Blackbird, Brewer's

SCIENTIFIC NAME: *Euphagus cyanocephalus*

DESCRIPTION: The males, which measure $7^1/_2$ to $9^1/_2$ inches long, are solid black with purplish-blue iridescent head and yellow eyes. The female is a dull gray-brown and has a dark eye. These birds walk with a distinctive jerk of the head.

HABITAT AND RANGE: Blackbirds can be found in open country, parks, and suburbs in the southern, central, and western parts of the United States. They often frequent farmyards, where they eat grain or insects found close to the surface of the soil.

The old nursery rhyme "Sing a song of sixpence, / A pocketful of rye, / Four and twenty blackbirds, / baked in a pie" was based on the fact that many centuries ago European peasants often ate the European blackbird.

Members of royalty were said to have used blackbirds as a source of amusement at banquets and parties. According to custom, they placed live blackbirds in a pie crust and when the "pie" was cut at the banquet, the birds would fly out, creating great amusement among the guests.

The symbolism of the blackbird is mixed. Black, of course, usually signifies death and evil, but the general symbolism for these birds connects them to everlasting life. As a result, the blackbird was sometimes considered symbolic of the struggle between good and evil, between body and soul. This bird is sometimes seen in paintings of the Mother and Child as a foreshadowing of the death of Christ.

According to the *Mondovi Bestiary*, the blackbird's song was heard but twice a year, symbolizing all those whose voices should be heard at confession (at least twice a year). Albertus Magnus wrote that the heart of the blackbird, if placed under the head of a sleeping man, would cause him to tell his innermost secrets.

Italian peasant lore holds that blackbirds were once all white but one winter the weather turned so nasty and cold that these birds had to find warmth in the chimneys of the town and were colored black by the soot. They have remained black to this day. Even now, some old folks call the days of January 31 and February 1 blackbird days.

The name *Euphagus* is from the Greek words for "good eater" (*eu*, for "good," and *phago*, meaning "to eat"). The species name *cyanocephalus* is from the Greek words *kaynos*, meaning "blue," and *kephale*, meaning "head," and refers to the color of this bird's head.

Brewer's Blackbird was named for Thomas Mayo Brewer, a physicist, journalist, politician, and ornithologist born in Boston in 1814. A friend of John James Audubon, Brewer was an enthusiastic bird lover.

When settlers first came to this country they found several different kinds of birds that

BREWER'S BLACKBIRD

looked like the European blackbird, and thus called them by the same name. Through the ages, however, scientists have determined that the English blackbird and the American blackbirds actually belong to different genera and are not related.

One of the most common, and perhaps the most beautiful, of all the American blackbirds is the red-winged blackbird, *Agelaius phoeniceus*. The male of this species is black with bright red shoulder patches. The female and young are black streaked with brown. They are frequently found near water, either marshes, swamps, or wet meadows.

Northern Louisiana Indians tell how the red-winged blackbird got its color. A wicked man set fire to the marshes one day. A small blackbird rose up out of the flames to fly away and get help. The man was so angry, he threw a shell at the bird, causing its wings to bleed.

This species often raises two or three broods per season. Once the breeding season is over, they gather in flocks of thousands, or even hundreds of thousands or millions, to fly south to their wintering grounds.

A flock of this magnitude obviously causes much damage as they travel, for they feed on field crops.

COMMON NAME: Bluebird, Western

SCIENTIFIC NAME: *Sialia mexicana*

OTHER SPECIES: Eastern Bluebird (*Sialia sialis*) and mountain bluebird (*Sialia currucoides*)

DESCRIPTION: Measuring 5 1/2 to 7 inches in length, the male bluebird is bright blue on the wings, head, tail, and throat. The center of the back and underparts are rusty brown. The female is not as bright and has grayish markings. This species is very similar to the eastern bluebird, though the female of that species shows brown markings rather than gray. The mountain bluebird is bright blue above and a paler blue on its underneath parts; this species breeds in high mountain meadows. Its range extends throughout the western areas of North America, from Alaska south to central Mexico.

HABITAT AND RANGE: Western and eastern bluebirds prefer open woods and farmlands. Eastern bluebirds are found east of the Rocky Mountains from southern Canada south to the mountains of central Mexico. Western bluebirds are found in most states west of the Mississippi River. During the summer breeding season, the mountain bluebird can be found at elevations as high as 12,000 feet.

Thoreau wrote that "the bluebird carries the sky on its back," and indeed as these beautifully colored winged creatures softly glide across the sky it is as if they have captured a piece of the sky and brought it to earth.

Bluebirds, native only to North America, were admired and cherished by the first explorers who found them in the New World. But even before this time, native Americans showed great love and appreciation for the bluebird.

Navajo Indians consider the bird sacred because its feathers are the color of the sky and are representative of the southern direction. They regard bluebirds as heralds of the rising sun, the supreme image of God. The Navajos believe that two of these birds stand at the door of the house in which God dwells.

Pima Indians believe that bluebirds were at one time a dull gray color. One day a flock of these birds found a beautiful blue lake, high up in the mountains. The lake had no inlet or outlet, and the birds bathed in it for four days. On the fourth morning, when they emerged from the lake, they had no feathers. On the fifth morning, their feathers had grown back the brilliant blue color of the lake.

Bluebirds have long been considered harbingers of spring and a symbol of happiness, love, and hope.

The bluebird has often figured in song and verse. James Russell Lowell wrote in *Under the Willows*: "The Bluebird shifting his light load of song, / From post to post along the cheerless fence." The idea of the bluebird of happiness originated with a Belgian playwright, Maurice Maeterlinck, who wrote a play called *The Blue Bird*. This exciting, symbolic drama is about a small boy and girl who set out to find the bluebird of happiness.

The bluebird is so beloved in America that many states have chosen it as their state bird.

The eastern bluebird was selected as Missouri's state bird in 1927 and as the official bird of New York State in 1970. The mountain bluebird, found commonly in the mountainous regions of the west, is the state bird for both Idaho and Nevada.

In spite of the fact that it has few natural enemies, the bluebird population has decreased drastically over the past few decades—by as much as 90 percent, according to some experts. The primary cause of this decline is lack of breeding places. Bluebirds have always built their homes in the cavities of dead trees or wooden fence posts. They also need wide open spaces, a type of landscape not easy to find in these days of progress and development.

These small birds compete for nesting sites with the more numerous starlings and house sparrows, and more often than not, they lose the competition. In response to this, many people put up special nesting houses for bluebirds. Long lines of these houses are located along rural roadsides and are called bluebird trails.

Another possible reason for the decline of the bluebird population is that they are particularly sensitive to herbicides and pesticides. The combination of a lack of nesting sites and the injudicious use of chemicals in lawns and gardens is a situation that homeowners and bird lovers can certainly change. By putting up bluebird boxes and limiting the use of chemicals in the garden, it is possible to help increase their natural population.

Bluebirds are very particular about the sort of house they will nest in. The entrance hole to the house must be $1\,^1/_2$ inches in diameter. This gives ample room for the small bluebirds to enter but effectively keeps out starlings, who are notorious for stealing nesting sites.

The birdhouses should be situated in an open area amid scattered trees, but far away

WESTERN BLUEBIRD

from any buildings. It is generally accepted that bluebirds prefer their houses to face south or east, and that they prefer high ground to low.

The houses should be mounted at a height of 3 to 5 feet, measured from the ground to the base of the house.

Finding an appropriate nesting site is the responsibility of the male bluebird, but once found, this site must be approved by the female. When the male has chosen a site he proceeds to "sell" it to his mate. He will go in and out of the house repeatedly, singing during the entire performance. This may take a few hours or it may take days. Once she okays the site, the female sets to work building the nest itself, usually of pine straw or dry grass.

Bluebirds eat soft-bodied insects and fruit and can often be seen perched on a limb, shoulders hunched over, bill pointed downward, as they stand poised to dive and swoop for dinner.

COMMON NAME: **Bobolink**

SCIENTIFIC NAME: *Dolichonyx oryzivorus*

DESCRIPTION: The breeding plumage of bobolinks is very different from the way the birds look after the summer molt. In spring males are black and white with a yellowish head. Females are a pale yellow-brown streaked with black. The wings are long and pointed, the tail short. These birds measure 6 inches long and have a short, conical bill.

HABITAT AND RANGE: Bobolinks live in prairies and fields. They breed in North America from British Columbia, Manitoba, and Newfoundland south to northern California, Colorado, and Pennsylvania. They winter in South America.

The song of the bobolink has been described as joyous and bubbling. Each note is a different pitch, creating a tinkling musical sound. Thoreau wrote: "This flashing, tinkling meteor bursts through the expectant meadow air, leaving a train of tinkling notes behind."

Dr. Eugene Murphey of Augusta, Georgia, described it like this:

High over the valley, in the cool nights of September
One hears the call notes of migrating Bobolinks
Falling like golden coins gently dropped
On slabs of porphyry
Cink-clink, clink-clink . . .

BOBOLINK

Bobolinks feed on grain, seeds, and insects. When rice plantations were common in South Carolina, bobolinks caused much damage. As they migrated south, thousands of bobolinks would land in the rice fields and eat until they became fat and round. They were known locally as butterbirds, or ricebirds, and were considered quite delicious.

Damage to field crops was such a problem that bobolinks were excluded from the list of birds protected by the Federal Migratory Bird Law of 1913. As a result, they were killed by the tens of thousands and the original population has never recovered. Luckily, the demise of the bobolink is no longer a problem, as new laws prohibit its killing and there are few rice fields left in the American South to tempt these musical little birds.

Bobolinks need open fields to breed. In many areas of the country, the native populations of this bird have diminished due to lack of appropriate breeding space. The birds will return to the same general area year after year. Usually the males return about a week before the females.

Though the common name is probably an imitation of this bird's bubbling song, it has also been immortalized in the poem by William Cullen Bryant, "Robert O'Lincoln." The genus name *Dolichonyx* is from the Greek words *dolichos*, meaning "long," and *onyx*, meaning "claw," a description of the bird's foot. The species name *oryzivorous* is from the Latin *oryza*, "rice," and *vorare*, "to eat," referring to the bird's love of this grain.

The bobolink males tend to be polygamous, having as many as four females in their nesting territory.

COMMON NAME: Bobwhite, Northern

SCIENTIFIC NAME: *Colinus virginianus*

DESCRIPTION: This small, chicken-like bird measures 8 inches in length. It is brown with pale underparts. The male has distinctive black and white markings; the female appears all buff or brown.

HABITAT AND RANGE: Bobwhites frequent grassy areas such as pastures, fields, and open woodlands. In the United States they range from Wyoming and Minnesota south to southern Texas and Florida. Small populations can be found in Washington and Oregon.

NORTHERN BOBWHITE

The call of the bobwhite is distinctive and makes this bird relatively easy to identify in the wild. Except during the breeding season, bobwhites live in coveys of about twenty to thirty birds and protect their territory fiercely.

In the evenings when the birds prepare to roost, they take cover under shrubs or brush and the entire covey congregates in a circle, heads pointed outward, tails touching in the center. This not only allows each bird clear flight if danger threatens, but also helps keep the birds warm by conserving heat.

Bobwhites are very shy birds and are sometimes difficult to see in the wild.

After bobwhites mate, the pairs spend all their time together, feeding and roosting. They create the nest by pecking a small indentation in the dirt under a shrub or other vegetation, usually about 50 feet from an open field or clearing. The birds then pull in grass, moss, and pine needles to create the nest. The entire nest is generally built in two to three hours.

The genus name is a corruption of the Nahuatl Indian word *zolin,* meaning "partridge."

Although the call of the bobwhite is usually identified with its name, farmers often say that the call of this bird actually sounds like "more wet" and is a promise of impending rain. Bobwhites often have a difficult time finding sufficient food during the winter months and greatly benefit from generous bird lovers who keep their feeders filled.

Being plentiful over a wide geographic range, bobwhites are considered a favorite game bird.

COMMON NAME: Bunting, Indigo

SCIENTIFIC NAME: *Passerina cyanea*

OTHER SPECIES: Lazuli bunting (Passerina amoena), painted bunting (Passerina circis)

DESCRIPTION: The indigo bunting measures about 5 1/2 inches long and has a small bill. The males are bright, iridescent blue when seen in the sunlight but otherwise look black. The bird will appear different shades of color in different kinds of light. The females are a drab brown above, paler beneath.

The lazuli bunting is slightly smaller, the male appearing bright blue with a light reddish brown breast and white belly and wing bars. The females look much like the indigo bunting but have wing bars.

The painted bunting measures 5 1/2 inches long and is brightly colored. The underparts and rump are red, the head is purple with a red eye ring, and the back is green.

INDIGO BUNTING

HABITAT AND RANGE: Indigo buntings are found in abandoned fields and clearings throughout the eastern part of the United States with the exception of Florida.

The lazuli bunting is found in overgrown pastures and weedy areas in the western United States and Canada from Saskatchewan south to western Oklahoma and westward.

The painted bunting frequents hedgerows, thickets, and areas covered with low brush. They are also sometimes found in swampy areas that supply sufficient cover.

The painted bunting takes cover in dense thickets, hoping to hide its circus-bright plumage. In some areas this bird is known as the nonpareil ("without equal"). Both indigo and painted buntings were at one time caught and sold as caged songbirds, a practice that is now, fortunately, illegal.

The indigo bunting's wings, which are actually black, have no blue pigment in them. The diffraction of light through the wings makes them appear blue.

During the summer, buntings live in pairs. As temperatures cool in autumn, though, they tend to congregate in flocks. The lazuli and indigo buntings have been known to interbreed but they do so rarely, keeping the two separate species intact.

The bunting was not always held in high esteem. In England during Shakespearean days, the bunting was thought to be a rather worthless bird. In Shakespeare's *All's Well That Ends Well*, Bertram says of Parrolles, "I took the lark for a bunting." A popular proverb of Elizabethan days said that "A goshawk begets not a bunting."

Although the bunting was often ridiculed in the field, it was nevertheless prized on the table in Elizabethan times and was often served at important banquets.

The genus name *Passerina* is a diminutive form for "sparrow." The species name *cyanea* is from the Greek word *kyanos,* meaning "blue." The common name lazuli is from the Latin word for the origin of the blue stones. The species name, *amoena,* means "delightful" or "charming."

The name for the painted bunting, *ciris,* comes from the Greek myth in which Scylla was transformed into a bird called the keiris.

The snow bunting, *Plectrophenax nivalis,* is in a different genus altogether. It is larger than other buntings, measuring between 6 and 7$\frac{1}{4}$ inches long. In summer the males are white with a black back. The females are white streaked with black. During winter months, both males and females are brownish underneath but white on top.

The snow bunting is found throughout the Arctic tundra in North America and spends its winters on beaches or grasslands. Flocks of snow buntings are sometimes found on beach parking lots.

Snow buntings have been called a variety of names including snowflake, snowbird, snow lark, and whitebird. These hardy little birds breed farther north than any other land bird.

The lark bunting, *Calamospiza melanocorys,* is the state bird of Colorado. John Burroughs wrote in *Far and Near.*

The only one of our winter birds that really seems a part of the winter, that seems to be born of the whirling snow, and to be happiest when storms drive thickest and coldest, is the Snow Bunting, the real snowbird. . . . Its twittering call and chirrup coming out of the white obscurity is the sweetest and happiest of all winter bird sounds. It is like the laughter of children. . . . It is ever a voice of good cheer and contentment.

In far northern countries the sound of the snow bunting is like a song of hope and life. These birds can withstand even the coldest winters and sing cheerfully as they brave the cold.

NORTHERN CARDINAL

COMMON NAME: Cardinal, Northern
SCIENTIFIC NAME: *Cardinalis cardinalis*

DESCRIPTION: Male cardinals are bright red with a crest and a black face and measure 8 to 9 inches long. The females are a soft brown color with an orangish crest and wings and a nearly white abdomen. The orange bill is short and stout.

HABITAT AND RANGE: Cardinals are found in yards and gardens, in woodland edges and in thickets throughout the eastern United States from the Dakotas south to the Gulf Coast and eastward.

The brilliant plumage of the cardinal makes this bird one of the easiest to identify. Though the female is much less colorful, the unusual orangish tinge to her crest and wings also makes her identification easy.

Just how did the cardinals come to be so beautifully colored? The Cherokee Indians tell the following tale:

A raccoon came upon a wolf one day in the forest and, in passing, made several insulting remarks to the wolf. The wolf became angry and began chasing the raccoon, who only laughed and ran swiftly through the forest. Finally the raccoon came to a tree beside a river and without missing a step, quickly climbed up and stretched out on a limb overlooking the water.

When the wolf came to the river he saw the reflection of the raccoon and jumped into the water after him. Once he realized his mistake, he began struggling toward land. When he finally pulled himself ashore, exhausted, he lay down on the bank of the river to rest and was soon sound asleep.

As nimbly as he had climbed up, the raccoon scrambled down from the tree and cautiously approached the sleeping wolf. Quickly he took mud from the river and flung it into the wolf's eyes and then ran into the forest.

When he awoke the wolf could not open his eyes and had to ask for help from a small brown bird sleeping close by. The little bird easily removed the mud from the wolf's eyes. The wolf was so grateful that he showed the little bird a magic pool of red.

The happy bird jumped into the pool and swam all around, being careful not to let the red paint get into his mouth. He then called his mate so that she, too, could become a beautiful red color. But by the time she got there almost all of the paint was gone and she could only add a little color to her wings and breast and crest.

And from that time on, the male cardinal has been all red, except for around his mouth, and the female has had to be content with her brown color and just a blush of red.

The Cherokee believe that the cardinal is the daughter of the sun.

A popular superstition suggests that if you see a cardinal flying toward the sky, it will bring you good luck. If he is flying toward the ground, however, bad luck is on the way.

Cardinals mate for life and will inhabit the same general vicinity for several years, often raising three or four broods during the breeding season. They are highly protective of their territory and will chase off other birds. When cardinals see their reflection in windows or glass doors, they often mistake it for another bird and vigorously attack the image over and over.

These birds sometimes feed on insects, including pests such as the Rocky Mountain locust and the Colorado potato beetle. The mainstay of their diet, however, is seeds and they often frequent winter bird feeders. Although cardinals were originally considered a southern bird, the species has greatly

extended its range northward and westward, thanks mainly to the profusion of backyard winter bird feeders.

Cardinals were named for the rich, bright red color found in the males, the same color as the robes worn by the cardinals of the Catholic Church. (The word *cardinal* is from the Latin *cardo,* meaning "hinge." The cardinals of the Church were so important to the Pope that many essential matters were dependent on, or "hinged" on, their decisions.) Cardinals are also known as redbirds and Virginia nightingales.

Cardinals have been chosen as the state bird by seven states: Illinois, Indiana, Kentucky, North Carolina, Ohio, Virginia, and West Virginia.

COMMON NAME: Chickadee, Black-capped
SCIENTIFIC NAME: *Parus atricapillus*
OTHER SPECIES: Mountain chickadee (*Parus gambeli*)

DESCRIPTION: These small birds are only 5 to 5³/₄ inches long. The top of the head, or "cap," is black, as indicated by the name. The throat is also black. The side of the head is white, with dull white underparts, and the back is gray.

The mountain chickadee, found throughout the western parts of the United States and Canada, looks similar to the black-capped, with the exception of a thin white line above the eye.

HABITAT AND RANGE: Chickadees prefer to nest in woodland areas, in cavities such as found in a hollowed log or stump or in a birdhouse. During winter months these birds are often found in suburban areas, where bird feeders are abundant. Black-capped chickadees breed across southern Canada and the northern United States from Alaska south to New Jersey, Missouri, and northern California.

Tirelessly cheerful, chickadees capture the hearts of bird lovers everywhere they visit. Seemingly full of personality, little chickadees are quite easy to tame. Bird lover John Woodcock wrote in 1913 that he had a chickadee so tame that it would perch on the bill of his hat and often swing, head down, to take a ride.

The chirpy call of the chickadee was sometimes thought to sound like "Spring's soon!" or "Sweet weather!"; thus the chickadees were considered harbingers of spring. John Burroughs wrote that the "chickadee has a voice full of unspeakable tenderness and fidelity."

The Cherokee Indians, who called the chickadee *tsikilili,* considered it a bringer of news. When a chickadee perched near the house, it was thought that a long absent friend would soon be heard from or that an enemy was plotting to get you. The chickadee is reported as saving the life of Tom Starr, once a noted solitary figure of the Cherokee Nation of the West. When Starr heard the chirpy call of this small bird, he realized he was being followed and managed to escape to safety.

When in danger, the chickadee has been known actually to spit with a small, sharp explosive sound.

The species name *atricapillus* is from the Latin words *altris*, meaning "black," and *capillus,* "hair of the head," and is descriptive of the appearance of this small bird. Unlike many other kinds of birds, chickadees do not migrate south during the winter and are one of the birds seen most frequently in the northern part of the country during the cold months. Although it weighs just one-half

BLACK-CAPPED CHICKADEE

ounce, the chickadee manages to stay alive during frigid weather by puffing out its feathers for extra insulation.

Many northern bird lovers are convinced that if they don't keep feeders filled during winter months, their chickadees will die. Yet researchers have found that they get only about 20 to 25 percent of their food from feeders. Mostly they eat from woods and fields.

This situation changes dramatically, however, when the mercury falls below 10 degrees Fahrenheit. Studies indicate that the survival rate of chickadees in these temperatures almost doubled when they had access to bird feeders. During cold weather these tiny birds need twenty times more food than they do in summer.

Chickadees belong to the same family as the tufted titmouse, *Parus bicolor.* Both are considered sociable birds and are often seen flocking together. These two species have a similar diet, consisting of seeds and insects. Chickadees often hang upside down from tree branches to feed on small insect eggs and larvae.

They will also congregate with other kinds of birds during the winter months and, together with woodpeckers, kinglets, and nuthatches, will form a loose flock moving through woods and fields.

The black-capped chickadee is the state bird of both Massachusetts and Maine.

BROWN-HEADED COWBIRD

COMMON NAME: Cowbird, Brown-headed
SCIENTIFIC NAME: *Molothrus ater*

DESCRIPTION: Cowbirds are 6 to 8 inches long and have a short, sparrow-like bill. The male is black with a lustrous brown head; the female is uniformly brown.

HABITAT AND RANGE: Cowbirds frequent suburban areas, fields, and agricultural lands throughout the United States.

Cowbirds in this country originally followed herds of bison or cattle (thus the common name) across the prairies and plains. As forests were cleared for homes and development, the range of this bird increased until it could be found from coast to coast.

The spread of this bird species is unfortunate, since it is a destructive nest or brood parasite and has caused a great decline in the populations of many species of smaller birds.

Because of their somewhat nomadic lifestyle, cowbirds do not stop and build a nest and raise a brood in one site. Instead, the female birds deposit an egg in the nest of some other (usually smaller) bird such as a warbler or vireo, leaving it to be hatched and raised by foster parents. The cowbirds are not particular as to where they leave their eggs; they have been known to lay eggs in nests of over 200 other species. Although the cowbird egg is sometimes rejected or covered with a new nest lining, it usually hatches and the young cowbird is raised along with the young of the host bird.

Cowbird eggs are usually larger and therefore tend to hatch sooner than the other eggs, and are generally larger than the young of their hosts, so they receive the greatest amount of food and attention from the foster parents and often even crowd out their nestmates. Once the cowbird leaves the nest, it finds and joins a flock of its own species.

In some woodland areas, several species of small songbirds have been nearly exterminated because of this destructive habit of the cowbird.

The genus name *molothrus* is probably a misspelling of the Greek word *molobros*, meaning "parasite," "vagabond," or "tramp," referring to the unsavory reputation of the cowbird. The common name cowbird is from cowpen bird, a name given by the English naturalist Mark Catesby. He wrote that "they delight much to feed in the pens of cattle, which has given them their name."

AMERICAN COOT

COMMON NAME: Coot, American

SCIENTIFIC NAME: *Fulica americana*

DESCRIPTION: A slate gray bird measuring nearly 15 inches long at maturity, the coot is characterized by a white bill and greenish legs.

HABITAT AND RANGE: Coots can be found throughout the continent from southern Canada to northern South America. They are aquatic birds, preferring open ponds and marshes, though they can also be found in saltwater inlets during winter months.

In *De Bestiis* it is written that the "coot is very intelligent and the most prudent of all birds. It neither eats cadavers, nor gads about from one place to another, but remains in one place, staying there until the end and finding there its food and rest."

The coot's solitary habits caused it to be referred to as a hermit and its nest a hermitage. The heart of the coot was once thought to be an effective cure for epilepsy.

Coots were once considered birds of beauty and honor, and many royal families included them in their coats of arms. This favorable view of the coot did not persist. Popular opinion today indicates an entirely different view of this water bird. "Silly old coot" and "crazy as a coot" suggest that some folks believe the coot to lack intelligence. "Bald as a coot" is an expression that was used even during medieval times and is a reflection of the physical appearance of the bird rather than of its character.

Coots feed both in the water (on aquatic plants) and on land (on grain, seeds, and grass). When feeding in the water, they often congregate near ducks and other waterfowl, eating aquatic plants and animals these birds have stirred up.

There are many common names for this bird. They include marsh hen, mud hen, water chicken, pond hen, white bill, hen bill, crow-blue Peter, splatter, shuffler, pelick, and pull-doo.

Both the common and generic names of this bird probably come from the word *soot,* a reference to its dark color. The Latin word for soot is *fuligo.*

Some species of coots live on a remote island that is completely lacking in natural predators for them. These coots have felt so safe for so long that, through the process of evolution, they have actually lost the ability to fly.

SANDHILL CRANE

COMMON NAME: Crane, Sandhill
SCIENTIFIC NAME: *Grus canadensis*

DESCRIPTION: Sandhill cranes are 3 to 4 feet tall with distinctively long neck and legs. Most of the body appears gray with a bright red patch on the crown. In flight it is distinguishable from the heron, as it flies with its neck outstretched.

HABITAT AND RANGE: This species prefers ponds and marshes in the prairies and tundra. It can be found in the most northern parts of Siberia, Alaska and the Arctic Islands, in parts of the Pacific Northwest, the Great Lakes states, and the Gulf states, from Florida to Texas.

The call of the crane has been described as the voice of nature—untamed, wild and free. Because of the volume of sound this bird can produce, the voice of the crane can be heard long after a noisy flock has flown past.

The Eskimos of northwestern Alaska tell the following tale of the cranes:

One cold autumn day long ago, the cranes began to prepare to fly south. As they gathered in a huge flock, they saw a beautiful young girl. They coveted her loveliness and finally decided to take her with them. Surrounding her, they lifted her on their widespread wings and carried her away. When she began to cry for help, they all flew close together, drowning her small voice with their mighty cries. So today, when the cranes fly close together, sounding their loud trumpet calls, it is time for all Eskimo children to come inside and stay close to their family.

In another story about migrating cranes, reported by Ernest Ingersoll in *Birds in Legend, Fable, and Folklore,* we find the suggestion that small birds often "hitched a ride" with bigger birds like the crane or the stork. Not only did the small birds get a free ride, but it was thought that the bigger birds benefited as well, for they like their little guests who by their merry twitterings help to kill the time on the long voyage.

Another ancient belief about migrating cranes is that they swallow a stone before they leave. This stone acts as ballast, keeping the cranes on course even in heavy winds. The stone regurgitated was thought to be a touchstone for gold.

For many centuries it was believed that cranes waged wars against the Pygmies. Milton described the Pygmies as "that small infantry warred on by cranes."

When they rested at night, the cranes were thought to have placed a sentry who would stand with one leg bent, a stone in its claw. If danger approached it would drop the stone and warn the others. This legend was so prominent that when cranes were depicted in English heraldry, they were always shown with a stone in one claw. This image became symbolic of vigilance.

Genealogy became an interest and passion among the British after the Norman conquest. A branching family tree, when written on paper, was referred to as a *pied de grue,* French for "foot of the crane." From this expression came the term pedigree.

One of the more intriguing characteristics of the crane is its mating dance. These big, awkward birds leap and dance with feet and wings thrown forward, all the time emitting loud croaking calls.

Marjorie Kinnan Rawlings wrote in her masterpiece *The Yearling*: "The cranes were dancing a cotillion as surely as it was danced at Volusia. . . . In the heart of the circle several moved counterclockwise. . . . The outer circle shuffled around and around. The group in the center attained a slow frenzy."

Several ancient cultures associated this ring dance with the cycle of the seasons. It was believed that spring had arrived when the cranes appeared. A ritualistic crane dance was performed to symbolize both fertility and death.

The crane, along with the mythical phoenix, is often referred to in Chinese legend. The black crane was thought to reach an old, old age, and thus became symbolic of longevity. The crane is often pictured under a pine, another symbol of age. In some cultures it was believed that the souls of the dead rode on a crane's back to heaven. In Chinese mythology, the immortal souls of the sages rode in a chariot pulled by a crane.

Cranes held captive in zoos have lived as long as eighty years. It is estimated that one of these large birds may live thirty to fifty years in the wild.

The name crane comes from an old Celtic word, *garan*, meaning "calling" or "crying out" and refers to the bird's distinctive song.

The whooping crane is much larger than the more common sandhill crane. The adults are white with black wing markings and spots of red on the crown and cheeks. Once common in many areas, the whooping crane was killed off so efficiently that at the low point of the population, only eleven birds remained alive in the world. Today that number has slowly increased, with hopes that the population will continue to recover. Every year a few eggs from the whooping crane are moved to the nest of a sandhill crane and left for this bird to raise.

COMMON NAME: Crossbill, Red

SCIENTIFIC NAME: *Loxia curvirostra*

DESCRIPTION: There is no mistaking the little sparrow-sized crossbill; its small bill is, as the name suggests, crossed at the tip. This bird measures $5^{1}/_{4}$ to $6^{1}/_{2}$ inches long. The male is a dull red, the female a drab gray-brown.

HABITAT AND RANGE: These birds are found most often in coniferous forests. Their range is difficult to determine, since they are sporadic visitors. They are sighted in an area in large numbers, and then are not seen there again for several years. In the West they have been spotted from southern Alaska south to southern California, and in the East from Quebec south to the North Carolina mountains.

RED CROSSBILL

The unusual configuration of the crossbill's beak has been explained in various legends. One of the best known is told in both Sweden and Ireland: When Christ was on the cross, the little crossbill tried valiantly to remove the nails from His hands. As it did so, its beak became twisted with its efforts. Longfellow phrased it this way:

> *Stained with blood and never tiring*
> *With its beak it doth not cease,*
> *From the Cross't would free the Saviour*
> *Its creator's son release.*

Crossbills feed almost exclusively on conifer cones. The unusual configuration of the bill makes it easier for crossbills to extract the seeds. They insert the closed bill inside a cone, then open their mandibles. This movement tears out the scales, leaving the seeds at the base. The muscles responsible for this action are so developed that crossbills can splinter solid wood with their bill.

Crossbills are nomadic and do not seem to be tied to any one locale. They stop and nest sporadically and create a colony wherever food is plentiful. The first red crossbill nest found in the United States was spotted in New York in April 1875, and they have not been seen breeding there since that time.

Because most seeds are found in the colder months, they even sometimes nest and raise a brood in the dead of winter. They have been found to nest during every month of the year. Crossbills found farther south than their normal range are thought to be a sign that the coming winter will be unusually harsh.

It was once believed that a crossbill kept nearby in a cage could cure colds and rheumatism—but only a bird whose mandibles were bent to the right could cure men, and one whose mandibles were bent to the left could cure women.

The unusual configuration of the bill has given rise not only to the common but also to the scientific names for this bird. The genus name *Loxia* is from the Greek *loxias*, which was an epithet given to Apollo, whose oracles were often puzzling or obscure—in other words, not straight. The word *loxos* means "oblique," or "deviating from a straight line."

COMMON NAME: Crow, American

SCIENTIFIC NAME: *Corvus brachyrhynchos*

DESCRIPTION: Crows are relatively large black birds measuring 17 to 21 inches long. The have a long, stout bill and a fan-shaped tail. The call of the crow is a harsh "caw-caw."

HABITAT AND RANGE: Crows are most often seen on farmlands and in residential areas and woodlands. Their range extends throughout the United States and the southern half of Canada.

Every country seems to have a common crow, and everywhere this bird is found, it is named for its raucous and shrill cry. The Anglo-Saxon word meaning "to crow" was *crawan*. In German the name is *Krähe*. In Swedish it is *kraka*. The Dutch word is *kraai* (pronounced *cry*).

Although the call of the crow is neither pleasant nor musical, these birds are considered songbirds because of the way their voice box is constructed.

Perhaps because this bird is so common, much superstition and legend has developed around the crow. For example, finding a dead crow in the road is supposed to give one good luck.

In England it was thought that to see a crow would ward off evil spirits. In Wales, it was considered unlucky if a crow crossed your path. But if two crows passed in front, the situation changed, as in "Two crows I see, good luck to me."

The direction the crows were flying also seemed important. In New England superstition it was unlucky to see two crows flying together toward your left.

In ancient Rome, crows were used for divination. A character in the *Asinaria,* by Plautus, a Roman playwright of the third century B.C., says, "The woodpecker and the crow on my right, the raven as well on my left. They are persuading me to do it."

One crow over the house meant a death there within the year, as indicated by the old country saying "A crow on the thatch, soon death lifts the latch."

The number of crows seen will tell the future: "One for sorrow, two for mirth, three for a wedding, four for a birth."

If a crow flew by with his mate at a wedding, the couple could look forward to a long and prosperous life together. If, however, a single crow flew across, it was believed that the couple would soon be separated.

French peasants say that bad priests become ravens, bad nuns become crows. The Greeks had an expression "Go to the crows," which was the equivalent of "Go to hell." The Romans used the phrase "to pierce a crow's eye" to mean that something was nearly impossible to do. The soul of Arthur of the Round Table is said to survive in the form of a crow, though some say it is a puffin.

The *Ch'un Ch'iu,* a Chinese history writ-

AMERICAN CROW

ten by Confucius, says that the "spirit of the sun is a crow with three legs." The crow was believed to have appeared with three legs because in Chinese mythology the number three is symbolic of light and good, of which the sun is the essence.

Many Native American tribes considered the crow sacred. It was thought that the crow brought the first grains and vegetables to man from the gods. The crow was used as an honored symbol of the Ghost Dance, an important ritual in which the tribe prepared for the return of peace and abundance on earth.

Crows appear in several colorful expressions in English, such as "to eat crow," which means to make a difficult apology or confession. (While young crows are said to be tender and tasty, old crows are tough and foul tasting.) "As the crow flies" refers to the shortest distance between two points. A "crow's nest" is the term for a lookout spot at the top of a ship's mast.

Although today a person might say, "I have a bone to pick with you," meaning that he wants to discuss a bit of unpleasant business with someone, originally the expression was "I have a crow to pick with you." And then there are "crow's feet," the network of small wrinkles found at the corner of the eyes of older people. Frederick Locker wrote of his grandmother:

Her locks as white as snow,
Once shamed the swarthy crow;
By-and-by
That fowl's avenging sprite
Set his cruel foot for spite
Near her eye.

During their molt in midsummer, crows are quiet and subdued. European peasants believed that it was during this time that the crows had to go to the Devil and pay tribute with some of their feathers.

The Audubon Society Field Guide describes crows as being "intelligent, wary, virtually omnivorous, and with a high reproductive capacity."

Because crows are particularly fond of young corn, farmers hate these birds and have developed the old-fashioned straw man to scare them away. In Wales, farmers would tie dead crows to their fences to ward off predators, thus the name "scarecrow."

In addition to corn, crows also eat a tremendous variety of foods, including fruit, seeds, grubs, and even eggs from other birds. Crows are wily creatures that work together. While several are feeding together, one stands guard and voices a warning call when danger approaches.

These birds can make good pets if tamed while young and can even be taught to mimic the human voice.

YELLOW-BILLED CUCKOO

COMMON NAME: Cuckoo, Yellow-billed

SCIENTIFIC NAME: *Coccyzus americanus*

DESCRIPTION: These birds are 11 to 13 inches long, have long tails, and are slender. They are generally brown above and white below, with large white spots on the underside of the tail and splotches of rusty color on the wings. The bill is slightly curved; the lower part of it is yellow.

HABITAT AND RANGE: Cuckoos prefer habitats where they have plenty of cover, such as overgrown fields and meadows, dense thickets and hedges. These birds breed in the United States from Minnesota and Maine south to Mexico and Florida. They winter in South America.

Wordsworth wrote: "O cuckoo! shall I call thee bird? / Or but a wandering voice?" The call of the cuckoo is so distinctive that it has given this bird its common name in many different languages. In Poland the name is *kukulka;* in France it is *coucou*. There are 127 different species of cuckoos found in many different countries throughout the world.

Other names for the yellow-billed cuckoo are rain crow, rain dove, storm crow, chow-chow, and kow-kow. The reason for these names is the habit of the bird of making unusual sounds before summer storms hit. The two latter names are imitations of this sound.

The yellow-billed cuckoo is a shy, furtive bird, rarely seen. It feeds voraciously on hairy caterpillars and is useful in keeping these pests in check.

The breeding habits of European cuckoos are considered particularly antisocial. The mother cuckoo lays her eggs in other birds' nests, and when the cuckoo chick hatches, it immediately burrows its way to the bottom of the nest. When any nestmates or unhatched eggs roll on top of its back, the cuckoo chick instinctively pushes them out of the nest.

The mother cuckoo chooses host birds whose eggs closely match those of her own. Neither cuckoo found in the United States (the yellow-billed or the black-billed) displays this behavior.

In Europe, where the birds do not build their own nests, to call someone a cuckoo was to call him lazy. Chaucer referred to the cuckoo as murderous. In the United States a cuckoo is a crazy person.

Cuckoos were also thought to be able to tell the future, as indicated by a Yorkshire nursery rhyme:

Cuckoo, cherry tree,
Come down and tell me
How many years afore I dee?

In Germany girls would ask the cuckoo how many years it would be before they would get married or how many children they would have. The number of calls that the cuckoo returned would be the answer to their question.

In Northumberland it was thought unlucky to hear the first cuckoo while walking on a road. In Germany and England, however, it was considered lucky to have money in one's pocket when one first heard cuckoo. If a person jingled coins in his pocket while hearing a cuckoo and made a wish, the wish would be granted. An English proverb puts it this way: "Turn your money when you hear the first cuckoo and you'll have money in your pocket until he comes again."

In Sweden it was believed that a cuckoo calling from the north meant sorrow, from the east, consolation, from the south, death, and from the west, good luck. A common cuckoo superstition in England held that to spot this bird flying overhead foretold death.

Cuckoos have always been considered weather-wise, especially gifted at predicting rain. Illustrations of Hindu myths show the cuckoo standing in front of the sun when it was hidden behind clouds, thus representing a cloudy day.

Cuckoos are always associated with the summer season. An English poem states it this way:

In April come he will.
In May he sings all day,
In June he'll change his tune,
In July he'll fly,
In August go he must.

Or, in other words, "A cuckoo song is a summer song."

The cuckoo was an ingredient in a traditional antidote for the bite of a mad dog. This concoction was made up of dung of badger, a cuckoo, and a swallow.

COMMON NAME: Dove, Mourning

SCIENTIFIC NAME: *Zenaida macroura*

OTHER SPECIES: White-winged dove (*Zenaida asiatica*), Inca dove (*Columbina inca*), ground dove (*Columbina passerina*)

DESCRIPTION: Mourning doves are a soft brown color and measure about 12 inches long. The tail is long and pointed; the tail feathers are tipped with white.

Other kinds of doves found in the United States include the white-winged dove, found in desert and farmland areas of the Southwest during the summer. The Inca dove is found in farms and suburban areas in southern Texas and Arizona. The common ground dove looks like a miniature mourning dove, measuring only 5 to 6 inches long, and is found in woodlands and farms throughout the southern states from California east to South Carolina.

HABITAT AND RANGE: Mourning doves can be found in a wide range of habitats—seemingly anywhere except for marshy areas or dense forests. They seem to prefer open areas such as fields and lawns, as long as nearby trees and shrubs offer a place for cover. This species is found throughout the United States and breeds throughout the United States and Southern Canada.

The name mourning dove was given to this bird because of its low, soft coo, which sounds like a mournful cry.

Mourning doves are one of the most prolific and widespread of all American birds. Different states betray different attitudes about this bird. Some states designate it as a songbird and protect it as such. Other states consider it a game bird and allow hunters to pursue it.

The species name *macroura* is Greek for "long-tailed." The genus *Zenaida* was named for Princess Zenaide Charlotte Julie Bonaparte, a granddaughter of the emperor Napoleon. The name dove is from German *dubo,* meaning dark-colored bird.

The dove has always been associated with myth and superstition throughout the world. It figures prominently in legends and stories in many different countries and is symbolic in many different religions.

The dove is an important Christian symbol. It is often shown symbolizing the Holy Spirit and is sometimes depicted as descending on the Virgin Mary at the Annunciation. It is also frequently used in pictures with the Virgin and Child, and at Creation. It is sometimes used in funeral rituals, symbolic of the

MOURNING DOVE

triumph of Christian faith over death. In Malory's *Morte d'Arthur,* a dove appears on the Holy Grail as a symbol of the purity and piety of the castle.

In 1873 Mackenzie E. Walcott wrote, in his *Notes and Queries,* "The dove was regarded as the symbol of the Holy Spirit which came in the eventide of days, bringing safety and peace to the ark of Christ."

In the Jewish faith, white doves were an acceptable sacrifice for those who could not afford to give a lamb. Mohammed considered the dove to be of particular importance. The dove, he said, was the spirit who came to him to give him the counsel of God.

The dove, as a Western symbol of peace, is often shown with an olive branch in its beak. This tradition is usually associated with the story of the Great Flood, when Noah released a dove from the ark to find land. The practice of releasing shore-seeking birds to see if land was near was one commonly used by sailors.

In Japan the dove was considered a messenger of war. This dates back to a Japanese legend about the mythical hero, Yoritomo, who was being pursued by two of his enemies. Yoritomo hid in the hollow of a tree. As the enemies approached, two doves flew out of the hollow, and the men assumed that no one was there and passed by. Yoritomo, who later became shogun, declared the dove his bird of luck.

European peasants believed that the dove's first call of the new year was important. If it came from above, it would mean prosperity and good luck; if from below, bad luck.

Another superstition holds that when a girl hears the first call of a dove in spring, she must take nine steps forward and nine back and take off her right shoe. In it will be the hair of the man she is to marry.

When children ask what the birds say when they sing, they receive a variety of answers. Coleridge answered it this way:

Do you ask what the birds say? The sparrow, the dove,
The linnet and thrush say, "I love and I love!"

A popular superstition of the American Southwest holds that white-winged doves paint themselves about the face to attract a mate. At first glance this would seem to be true, for they often appear red around the mouth, as if they have used lipstick. In fact, the color is only a result of eating the ripe red pears from the saguaro cactus.

Doves and pigeons produce a rich, nutritious substance called pigeon milk for their broods. This is produced by glands in the adult's gullet. For the most efficient transfer of this substance from the adult to the nestling, a young bird actually puts its head inside the parent's mouth to get to the food.

MALLARD DUCK

COMMON NAME: Duck, Mallard

SCIENTIFIC NAME: *Anas platyrhynchos*

OTHER SPECIES: Wood duck (*Aix sponsa*), blue-winged teal (*Anas discors*), and northern pintail (*Anas acuta*)

DESCRIPTION: Wild ducks are classified into several different groups. These include dipping ducks, diving ducks, and perching ducks. Technically, a duck is the female, and a drake is the male. Although there are great differences among species of ducks, they all share certain characteristics. All are round and plump and are designed for life in the water. The feathers are kept waterproof by glands that secrete a special oil. A thick layer of down helps keep them bouyant and warm during cold weather.

The body of the duck is designed for swimming. The short legs are set far back on the body, making it awkward to walk but wonderfully efficient to swim. The feet are webbed, adding to the powerful swimming strokes of these birds.

Mallards are generally 20 to 28 inches long with a short, blunt tail. The males have a glossy green head with white neck ring, a chestnut brown chest, and a pale brown back. The female is mottled brown all over with an orange bill.

Male wood ducks are beautifully colored with a bright green crest, speckled chestnut chest, red bill, and bold white markings on the face.

Blue-winged teals are 14 to 16 inches long. As the name suggests, the wing of the male is characterized by striking blue and green feathers. The female is a uniform grayish brown with pale blue wing patches.

Northern pintail males are 25 to 29 inches long; the females are much shorter, measuring only 20 to 22 inches. The head of the male is brown marked with a thin, long, white stripe. The tail is long and slender with black feathers in the center.

HABITAT AND RANGE: Ducks are water birds and frequent ponds, lakes, and marshy areas. Mallards are found throughout the United States, including Alaska. Wood ducks are found in the eastern half of the country and in the Pacific Northwest. Blue-winged teals are generally found throughout the United States except for southeastern Texas and western New Mexico. Northern pintails are found in all areas of the country except for inland New England.

The Egyptians first domesticated ducks nearly 5,000 years ago, and the ancient Chinese are also known to have raised these birds.

Native Americans tell the following creation story:

Nesaru, the great sky spirit, had charge over all of creation. Below the sky there was a huge lake where two ducks swam—eternally at peace with one another and with all of creation.

One day Wolf-man and Lucky-man asked the ducks to dive and bring up mud to make the earth. The ducks agreed and dived deeper than they had ever been before. When they came out of the water, they had little bits of mud in their bills. From this mud Wolf-man made the prairie where all the animals could live and Lucky-man made hills and valleys where the Indians could hunt.

Scientists have discovered that baby mallards imprint on the call and voice of the mother but not necessarily on what she looks like.

The name duck came from the Latin word "to dive."

The slang term "ducky" used as a term of endearment dates back to the late 1500s. In the late 1800s and early 1900s "ducky" meant cute or attractive.

COMMON NAME: Eagle, Golden
SCIENTIFIC NAME: *Aquila chrysaetos*

DESCRIPTION: From the ground, a soaring eagle can be distinguished from other birds of prey by its great size, 35 inches or more in length, and by its long, rounded wings, which can span 7 feet. The adult is a uniform dark, rich, chocolate brown color with mottled white at the base of the fan-shaped tail. The golden neck feathers that give the bird its name are visible only at close range. Immature birds are dark below with white windows in the wings and a white tail with a broad black band at the tip. The eagle's heavy hooked bill is nearly as long as the head.

HABITAT AND RANGE: The golden eagle inhabits remote mountains, tundra, grasslands, and deserts. It breeds in the western mountain regions of the United States and Canada, and is less commonly seen east of the Mississippi River.

The nest, or aerie, is a large, bulky platform of sticks 5 to 8 feet across and is often built on inaccessible cliffs or in large trees. These massive nests can weigh more than a ton, and are often occupied for periods of seventy to a hundred years.

The golden eagle preys on rodents, ground squirrels, and other small animals.

This bird is sometimes known as the "booted" eagle, as its legs are feathered to the toes.

The eagle has been important in legend, symbolism, and mythology in many different cultures. It is a magnificent-looking bird, meriting both attention and admiration. In most cultures where the eagle is revered, it is symbolic of the sun or serves as the emblem for the sun deity.

Lagash was an important city in ancient Sumer (circa 3000 B.C.). The military emblem for this city was an eagle with wings and legs spread, head turned to the side. From this the double headed eagle was derived, an emblem that has appeared through the ages and even survives in modern European symbolism.

The eagle was the messenger for the Greek god Zeus. The Romans also revered the eagle, and it became the official emblem of Rome in 87 B.C.. The Roman eagle was always shown carrying lightning bolts in his claw. This dates back to a legend that says that when Jupiter (the Roman counterpart to Zeus), was getting ready for battle with the Titans, an eagle brought him his dart. From that time, the eagle was shown carrying thunderbolts, and was a symbol of power. To speak of the "eagles of Rome" was to speak of the military might of the Roman army.

The legendary migration of the Aztec Indians was thought to have ended when the

GOLDEN EAGLE

leaders saw a sign from their gods—an eagle perched on a prickly-pear cactus, strangling a serpent. They decided to settle in what was the Valley of Mexico in A.D. 1325. Cortés had the eagle and the serpent engraved on coins, and Mexico has kept this emblem to this day.

In 1782 the bald eagle was chosen as the bird emblem for the United States. In its right claw is a spray of olives, symbolic of peace, and in its left is a bundle of arrows, indicating unity.

Many members of Congress were against the choice of this bird. Most outspoken among them was Benjamin Franklin, who wrote of the bald eagle, "He is a bird of bad moral character. . . ." In spite of his protests, the eagle remains our national symbol.

How the eagle appeared and in what direction it was flying were of great importance to the superstitious of earlier days. When the eagle was lively and flew from the right to the left, it was considered a very good omen from the gods.

The golden eagle held special significance for the Plains Indians. It was thought to be the personification of bravery, and its feathers were considered a means of communicating with the spirits. Although the feathers were of enormous value, it was considered a sacrilege to kill eagles with a bow and arrow. Obtaining the feathers, then, involved much difficulty and danger. The Pueblo Indians sometimes trapped young chicks and kept them in cages until they were full grown. A mature eagle has twelve large tail feathers, all of which were dearly prized for war bonnets and ceremonial dances.

Shakespeare wrote of this bird: "The eagle does not stoop to catch flies." And William Blake wrote "The eagle never lost so much time as when he submitted to learn of the crow."

So smooth and symmetrical is this bird that a level board would fit snugly across the flat, outstretched wings of a soaring eagle.

The female eagle lays two eggs and immediately begins incubating after the first egg is laid rather than wait for both. The eggs hatch in sequence, and one sibling is invariably bigger than the other. The older eaglet often kills and eats the younger if food supplies are low.

GREAT EGRET

COMMON NAME: Egret, Great
SCIENTIFIC NAME: *Casmerodius albus*

DESCRIPTION: A magnificent, tall, white bird, the great egret has a long yellow bill and slender, black legs and is 35 to 40 inches long. The feathers all over are snowy white. During breeding season, additional long silky white feathers appear around the tail. Most egrets don't stretch their neck, but carry it in an S shape when in flight.

HABITAT AND RANGE: Great egrets live in marshy areas, both fresh- and saltwater, from Oregon to South America. These birds are commonly found wintering in coastal areas in the Southeast as far north as South Carolina, and along the Gulf Coast.

Many common names have been attributed to this stately bird, including American egret, common egret, large egret, and great white heron. In North America, it is now correctly called the great egret. *Casmerodius,* the genus name, is from two Greek words, *chasma* and *herodias,* which together mean "gaping heron."

The great egret suffered a tremendous decline in population during the years when it was hunted for its outstandingly beautiful plumage. Fortunately, strict enforcement of protection laws has resulted in its recovery.

The white feathers of this bird were worn by ball players among the Cherokee Indians as a sign of speed and luck. The feathers were also carried as a peace emblem in ancient times.

The great egret stalks shallow waters alone, feeding on fish, frogs, snakes, and crayfish. The snowy egret, *Egretta thula,* is small by comparison, only reaching 20 to 27 inches in height. Its bill and legs are black, the feet yellow. A distinctive yellow band goes from the bill to its eyes. Long, fancy plumes appear along the back during breeding season. This water bird lives in salt marshes and shallow coastal waters, ponds, and marshes down the East Coast from Maine to Florida, along the Gulf Coast, and in isolated spots in the West.

The breeding plumage of the snowy egret, like that of the great egret, was the prize of many hunters, causing its near extinction. Fortunately, this population, too, has recovered.

The cattle egret, *Bubulus ibis,* is well known for its symbiotic relationship with elephants, rhinos, and cattle in Africa. The egrets ride on the backs of these lumbering animals, occasionally pulling off ticks or other bothersome insects. In return, the large animals stir up vast quantities of grasshoppers and other insects, which the egrets promptly eat.

The first cattle egrets were discovered in the United States in April 1952. Later that same year, other cattle egrets were spotted in New Jersey and Florida.

PEREGRINE FALCON

COMMON NAME: Falcon, Peregrine
SCIENTIFIC NAME: *Falco peregrinus*

DESCRIPTION: About the size of a crow (approximately 15 to 20 inches long), peregrine falcons are dark gray above with an almost solid dark head, becoming more speckled on the back and wings. Lower parts are much paler. The area below the beak and the chest is white, the bill and feet yellow. This falcon, with its long, narrow tail and pointed wings, has rapid wingbeats.

HABITAT AND RANGE: Falcons live in open areas close to water, along rivers, and beside lakes. When migrating, they remain close to coastal areas. They breed in Alaska, northern Canada, south along the Rocky Mountains, and in parts of the eastern United States. They are sometimes seen during winter throughout Florida and in other eastern coastal regions.

In Japan the falcon as a symbol of victory dates back to the story of the mythical ancestor Jimmu Tenno. When he landed on the shore of the Japanese islands, a falcon is said to have flown toward him and landed on the bow of his ship. Since then, the falcon represents a successful undertaking.

The falcon adorned the Medal of Victory awarded to outstanding Japanese soldiers.

The name falcon is from the Latin word *falc,* or *falx,* meaning "sickle." This word refers to the shape of the bird's claws—not its bill.

In ancient Greece, falcons were considered sacred to the god Apollo.

The sport of falconry is the art of taming certain birds of prey and hunting game with them. Although this sport reached its zenith in Europe during the Middle Ages, it began far earlier than this. Drawings and small statues found in Egypt and Mongolia indicate that falconry is indeed an ancient art. Although many different kinds of birds can be trained, it is the falcon that is used most satis-factorily. During the Middle Ages, peasants used goshawks while knights and aristocrats used falcons.

Women hunted with smaller species of falcons, and hawking parties became special social occasions. The jargon of the falconer is full of words and phrases that are foreign to us today. To "bowse" means to drink, to "feak" is to wipe the beak of the bird after it eats, to "warble" means to stretch its wings. As with all birds of prey, the female is larger than the male and is the one used most often in falconry. A "cadge" is the perch on which the birds are carried to the field. The man who carried this was usually an older falconer and he was called the cadger—from which we get "old codger."

Peregrine falcons were often used by sport falconers. They are among the fastest flyers, sometimes reaching speeds of up to 180 miles per hour when attacking smaller flying birds. The beak of the peregrine falcon has a notch along the lower edge that fits neatly between the neck vertebrae of the birds it hunts.

The reputation of falcons as superior hunters was well established by the time Shakespeare wrote about the unnatural events surrounding Duncan's murder by Macbeth:

On Tuesday last,
A falcon, towering in her pride of place,
Was by a mousing owl hawk'd at and killed.

These falcons are extremely sensitive to pesticides, a situation that has severely reduced the natural population. Researchers have discovered that eating a single contaminated duck will cause complete infertility in a falcon.

For more information about falcons, contact:

The Peregrine Fund, Inc.
World Center for Birds of Prey
5666 West Flying Hawk Lane
Boise, ID 83709
208–362–3716

COMMON NAME: Finch, Purple
SCIENTIFIC NAME: *Carpodacus purpureus*

DESCRIPTION: A small sparrow-sized bird, the purple finch appears more red than purple. The head and rump are a distinct raspberry color, the end of the wings and tail a darker red. The female purple finch is nearly all brown streaked with white. Both male and female have conical bills.

HABITAT AND RANGE: Purple finches frequent gardens of suburban areas and mixed forests. They generally nest in conifers. Purple finches breed in Canada and parts of the United States and migrate south to the eastern half of the United States as well as the West Coast.

The genus name *Carpodacus* is from the Greek words *karpos,* meaning "fruit," and *dakos,* meaning "biting." It is believed that these birds eat berries of ornamental plants. Purple finches are partial to sunflower seeds and during the winter months frequent bird feeders.

The house finch, *Carpodacus mexicanus,* is similar to the purple finch. These birds lived in the western part of the country and were brought east as caged birds. Illegally sold as "Hollywood finches," they were popular items in pet stores until the National Audubon Society was able to put a stop to

PURPLE FINCH

this illegal sale of songbirds protected under the Migratory Bird Treaty. Many of these birds were released and managed to survive on Long Island. By the 1970s the house finch population had become established in the East and had spread southward to Georgia and North and South Carolina.

When British naturalist Charles Darwin traveled to the Galapagos Islands and began the study that would result in his theory of evolution, the finches he found on these remote islands were of particular interest to him.

The purple finch was chosen as the New Hampshire state bird in 1957.

COMMON NAME: Flicker, Common

SCIENTIFIC NAME: *Colaptes auratus*

DESCRIPTION: The common flicker is 12 to 14 inches long and has a conspicuous white rump patch and a brown back. The breast is a cream color with black spots; a wide black band crosses the top of the breast.

The common flicker species includes both the yellow- and red-shafted flicker and the gilded flicker. The yellow-shafted flicker is most often seen in the eastern United States. Viewed from below, the bright yellow underparts of the tail and wings are very noticeable. At close range the red crescent on the nape and the black moustache of the male are also apparent.

The red-shafted flicker of the western states shows pinkish red on the underparts of the tail and wings. This species has a red moustache.

HABITAT AND RANGE: The common flicker is a year-round resident of the United States. Its summer range includes Canada and Alaska to the tree line. Flickers inhabit aspen groves and open woodlands.

The gilded flicker is a resident of deserts in southeastern California and southern Arizona. In the Arizona desert it is frequently seen on saguaro cactus on which it also makes its nest.

There are about 132 common names for yellow-shafted flicker, one of the most popular of which is yellowhammer. The genus name *Colaptes* is from the Greek *kolaptes*, meaning "chisel." *Auratus* is from the Latin word for "golden." There are several

possibilities as to the origins of the name flicker. According to one account the word flicker means "one who strikes." Another suggestion is that it got its name from its "flick-flick-flick" call.

Flickers are actually a kind of woodpecker.

COMMON FLICKER

Unlike its tree-bound cousin, however, the flicker spends much of its time on the ground searching for ants. The chisel-like bill is sharply pointed, making it wonderful for dipping and digging in fallen tree trunks. The tongue of this bird, which extends a full 3 inches beyond its bill, is ideally suited for capturing ants. Yellowhammers also eat berries, fruits, ant eggs and larvae, insects, and spiders.

In the Old World, the yellowhammer was a name given to the yellow bunting and was believed to be the bird of the devil.

Adult male flickers have a stripe on either side of the bill that looks much like a moustache. This stripe is an identifying feature for sexes. Scientists conducted an experiment in which a "moustache" was taped to the bill of a female flicker. When her mate returned, he attacked her, thinking she was a rival male.

The yellowhammer is the state bird of Alabama. It was given this distinction in a former era by the Ladies' Memorial Association, as the Alabama soldiers of the Confederacy were known as "Yellow Hammers."

COMMON NAME: Flycatcher, Great Crested

SCIENTIFIC NAME: *Myiarchus crinitus*

DESCRIPTION: This bird measures about 9 inchs long and is approximately the size of a robin. It has rusty cinnamon wings, a tail with yellow underparts, and a gray throat and breast. The head and back are olive brown.

HABITAT AND RANGE: Flycatchers breed in deciduous woodlands throughout the eastern half of the United States.

The Cherokee Indians speak of an unusual bird with a forked tail that came to visit only rarely. Because the bird had red spots on it, it was thought to be not a bird but a transformed red-horse fish. One young Indian boy even reported seeing seven of them lined up on a branch still in the shape of a red-horse but with wings and feathers.

While it was in the area where the Cherokees lived, this bird helped the tribe, for it ate

tremendous numbers of hornets and even ate the larvae from the nests. This undoubtedly was the scissor tail or swallow-tailed flycatcher, which normally lives in Texas but sometimes strays eastward.

The genus name comes from two Greek words, *myia,* "fly," and *archon,* "ruler"—"ruler of flies." *Crinitus* is from the Latin for "hairy" or "crested." Neither the common nor the scientific name is altogether appropriate, for

GREAT CRESTED FLYCATCHER

this bird is not great in size nor is it crested.

The flycatcher gets its name from its voracious appetite for insects. These birds can often be found perched in the shade, watching patches of sunlight for unsusupecting prey. They are active, aggressive birds, frequently taking flight to catch dinner or to run off potential nest robbers, such as blue jays and crows.

The great crested flycatcher has been observed to weave a discarded snake skin into its nest to help ward off other predators.

COMMON NAME: Frigatebird, Magnificent

SCIENTIFIC NAME: *Fregata magnificens*

DESCRIPTION: The frigatebird is a large black seabird with a long, pointed tail and angular wings that show a prominent crook. The forked tail opens wide and is easily observed when the bird is maneuvering but appears folded together when the bird glides. Frigatebirds are the only seabirds that show a pronounced difference in coloration between the male and female. The male has a red throat patch that is often inflated during courtship. The female has a white breast and dark head. Both birds have a long, light-colored, hooked bill.

HABITAT AND RANGE: Generally confined to tropical areas, frigatebirds live in the Gulf of Mexico, the Florida Keys, Hawaii, and Baja California. They occasionally wander north along the Pacific Coast as far as Oregon.

Frigatebirds are among the largest of all seabirds, with a wingspread of almost 8 feet. Because their weight is small in proportion to their wing area, these birds can fly for days without landing. Although they are silent most of the year, adult birds sometimes emit a loud, haunting, whistling cry while breeding.

Because frigatebirds have a very small oil gland and almost no waterproofing in their plumage, they do not swim or land on water. To feed, they capture small fish on the wing from near the surface of the water. Only the tip of their bill touches the water, leaving but the slightest ripple on the surface.

Frigatebirds also sometimes rob prey from

MAGNIFICENT FRIGATEBIRD

other seabirds, a practice known as "klep-toparasitism." They patrol the shoreline intercepting inbound birds and then hound them until they cough up their fish. This practice earned them the common name, man-o-war bird.

At night these birds rest in trees along the shoreline. During breeding season they make stick platforms in trees and sometimes in rocky niches.

This bird was named for the eighteenth-century sailing warships called frigates.

COMMON NAME: Gnatcatcher, Blue-gray
SCIENTIFIC NAME: *Polioptila caerulea*

DESCRIPTION: The little gnatcatcher is only 4 inches long and resembles a mocking-bird. It is bluish gray on the back and head, and white below, with a long, dark tail and white eye-ring. The tail often twitches side-ways and is frequently cocked, like a wren's.

HABITAT AND RANGE: These birds inhabit many different areas, including moist forests and arid lands from coast to coast throughout the southern United States. They sometimes range as far north as Wyoming, New York state, and southern Ontario.

Its nest is a neat, deep cup made of plant pieces, grasses, and strips of bark all held together with silk from spiderwebs. The outside of the nest is carefully covered with pieces of lichen, perhaps to help camouflage the nest, which may be found anywhere from 2 to 70 feet up in a tree.

Gnatcatchers seem to be forever on the move, flitting up and down, in and out. To maintain such constant activity, these small birds need an enormous amount of food, which they catch on the wing. This species feeds almost entirely on insects.

Gnatcatchers are seemingly unafraid of intruders and will not hesitate to attack birds much larger than themselves who barge into their territory. The male and female take turns sitting on the nest incubating the eggs and never try to be the least bit secretive about where the nest is. The male seems to carry on a constant song throughout the breeding season.

The genus name *Polioptila* is from two Greek words, *polios,* meaning "hoary" or "gray," and *ptilon,* meaning "feather."

BLUE-GRAY GNATCATCHER

AMERICAN GOLDFINCH

COMMON NAME: Goldfinch, American
SCIENTIFIC NAME: *Carduelis tristis*

DESCRIPTION: This small yellow bird has a conical bill, black cap and wings, and a notched tail. The female and young have an unstreaked back and breast. The body is olive-yellow fading to light yellow below with dark wings and tail. During breeding season the male is bright yellow with a white rump.

HABITAT AND RANGE: Goldfinches range from coast to coast, from southern Canada to northern Mexico. They are often seen feeding on weed seeds along the roadsides. When flushed, the flock will rise suddenly and fly with an undulating motion to the safety of a nearby field.

The poet T. S. Eliot wrote about what pleasure it was to ". . . Follow the dance of the goldfinch at noon." The bright plumage of the breeding males makes the sighting of the goldfinch unforgettable.

Goldfinches apparently do not like to fly over large bodies of water. During migration in the northern parts of the United States, they will often hesitate before crossing a major lake. Sometimes they will even start across and then return to shore to rest and feed until cold weather forces them to continue their journey.

Goldfinches, also known as wild canaries, love seeds and flowers, particularly dandelions, sunflowers, and thistles. The genus name, *Carduelis,* is from the Latin word *carduus,* which means "thistle." These birds even use the thistledown to line their nests. Goldfinches are so dependent on thistles and other weeds for food and nesting materials that they actually delay breeding until mid-to-late summer when seeds and thistledown are readily available. Because they breed so late in the year, goldfinches usually raise only one brood per season.

The name finch can be traced back to the German word *Fink,* which imitates the noise the birds make. The species name *tristis* is from the Latin for "sad," a reference to its voice.

Romans kept finches in cages, especially the bullfinch, which could be trained to sing. The Spanish artist Goya (1746–1828) painted Don Manuel Osorio de Zúñiga with a magpie on a leash and a cage full of European goldfinches. The Venetian artist Tiepolo (1696–1770) painted the Madonna of the Goldfinch, showing Mother and Child and a tiny goldfinch.

Iowa chose this as its state bird in 1933, New Jersey in 1935, and the state of Washington in 1951.

CANADA GOOSE

COMMON NAME: Goose, Canada
SCIENTIFIC NAME: *Branta canadensis*

DESCRIPTION: The Canada goose measures 25 to 45 inches long and has a wingspread of $5\frac{1}{2}$ feet. It is a large bird with a black head, bill, and neck and a bold, white cheek patch.

HABITAT AND RANGE: The Canada goose breeds across North America, from Alaska to eastern Canada and south to Mexico. It frequents many different types of bodies of water, including lakes, marshes, bogs, and sloughs.

One of Aesop's most famous fables is "The Goose with the Golden Eggs." In this story a man has a goose who begins to lay one golden egg every day. The man eventually becomes so greedy that he finally kills his goose to get at the source of the gold, only to find out that with the goose dead, there were no more golden eggs. An old English proverb sums it up this way: "Kill not the goose that lays the golden eggs."

In Egyptian mythology, a goose laid a golden egg, which became the sun. Still another story, from India, said that the Great Spirit laid a golden egg, which represents the sun. From this, Brahma, the Breath of Life, was born. The goose was also sacred to Woden, the Germanic god of storms.

Several folk and country sayings involve the goose. One of these says that "when it snows, the old lady is plucking her geese." A French proverb suggests that "it is a stupid goose that listens to the fox preach." And of course the English remind us that "sauce for the goose is sauce for the gander."

The name goose comes from the Old English *gos,* in which the *o* was pronounced long. The word was probably an imitation of the sound that these birds make. A male is called a gander, and babies are goslings. The Indian word for the Canada goose is *wawa.* The town of Wawa, Ontario, Canada, erected a 24-foot, 3,500-pound statue of the Canada goose to welcome visitors.

Geese are vegetarians. They eat grass, roots, and green leaves. Sometimes farmers will keep geese to help weed their fields. Because the geese do not like young cotton or strawberry plants, they are put on these fields to eat the grass that comes up. An added benefit was the instant fertilizer the geese spread as they wandered through the fields. Geese are actually better walkers than they are swimmers.

The Canada goose, which is the most common goose in the United States, flies in the well-known V pattern; they often honk loudly as they travel. The lead bird frequently changes places with others in the line, as it is more exhausting to fly in the lead position.

The most rare goose in the United States is the nene, which is native to the Hawaiian Islands. This bird suffered great reduction in its population because it was often killed by man, pigs, and dogs. Another rare species, the snow goose, breeds in northern Canada and Alaska. This is the goose of the popular Hans Christian Andersen fairy tale of the same name.

Geese have been domesticated for many centuries. Romans kept a flock of geese at the Temple of Juno inside Rome. In A.D. 390, when raiders tried to enter the city, geese raised an alarm. Once geese were a major source of commerce in Europe. They produced feathers for stuffing and quills for making into pens, and they were fattened for eating, particularly in the fall. Their eggs were also eaten and their fat used in cooking.

Five thousand years ago, geese were considered sacred birds and were sometimes symbolic of fertility. Wild geese, which mate for life, were taken as a symbol of marital fidelity.

Romans used the breastbone of a goose to predict the weather. It had to be from a goose hatched during the preceding spring. The bone is thin and full of spots, all of which supposedly had meanings. For example, if the spots were light colored and the bone transparent, wet weather was coming. An old country saying refers to this ancient superstition:

> *If the November goose-bone be thick,*
> *So will the winter weather be;*
> *If the November goose-bone be thin,*
> *So will the winter weather be.*

Old legends suggest that geese breed and grow in the shell of a barnacle, from which they drop as they mature; thus was born the idea of the barnacle goose. During the Middle Ages, geese were thought to grow on trees. A manuscript from an eleventh-century churchman showed goslings bursting forth from the fruit of a tree. Disputes about the classification of geese continued for a long time: In 1187, Giraldus Cambrensis, archdeacon of the Welsh Church, reprimanded priests in Ireland for eating barnacle geese during Lent because they were considered meat.

The Cherokee Indians believed that in the beginning of the world there was only one tobacco plant and that a goose stole it and carried it far away to the south. Eventually it was returned to the people by the tiniest hummingbird.

The idea of Mother Goose supposedly came from an early queen of France, the mother of Charlemagne, Bertha Goosefoot. She received this name for her big, floppy feet. After her death, peasants told stories about her and transformed her into the mythic Mother Goose.

Konrad Lorenz was one of the first scientists to experiment with imprinting, the learning mechanism that develops very early in an animal's life by which certain stimuli prompt specific behaviors. Lorenz suggested that baby geese would imprint on whatever they saw as soon as they hatched from the egg. To prove this, he carefully hatched goslings from the egg and himself served as their substitute mother. Since he was the first moving object the geese saw when they hatched, they imprinted on him and followed him around. He raised them to maturity.

The term *goose bumps*—also *goose pimples* and *goose flesh*—comes from the fact that these tiny lumps on the skin look like the bumpy skin of a plucked goose.

Aldo Leopold, the naturalist famous for his book *The Sand County Almanac,* spent his life in forestry, game management, and conservation. He once wrote, "One swallow does not make a summer, but one skein of geese, cleaving the murk of a March thaw, is the spring."

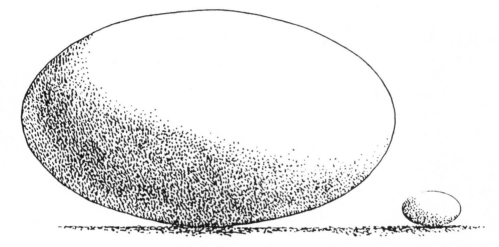

Relative sizes of goose egg and hummingbird egg

COMMON GRACKLE

COMMON NAME: Grackle, Common

SCIENTIFIC NAME: *Quiscalus quiscula*

DESCRIPTION: Large and black, and with a long, keel-shaped tail, the grackle measures 12 inches in length. In sunlight, the glossy black feathers sparkle with iridescence. The pale yellow eye of the adult is an outstanding characteristic, allowing even the amateur to identify this bird with no trouble. Females are smaller and duller in appearance.

HABITAT AND RANGE: The grackle breeds across Canada and the United States, from the foothills of the Rockies east to the Atlantic and south to Florida and Texas. They are rarely found west of the Rockies. Grackles prefer to stay near water and can often be seen close to rivers and streams. These birds also frequent urban areas, such as home gardens and city parks.

In 1918 the United States government passed the Migratory Bird Treaty Act, protecting migratory nongame birds. But certain species of birds that gather in tremendous numbers and cause serious damage to ornamental and agricultural crops were excepted from the act. Among these offenders are grackles. (In the spring of 1974, a flock of about ten thousand grackles, blackbirds, and starlings descended on Washington, D.C. Although authorities tried to drive them away with whistles, sirens, and lights, nothing worked, and much damage resulted.)

Grackles adjust their diet to whatever is available. In addition to agricultural crops and garden flowers and trees, grackles eat insects, seeds, fruits, frogs, and reptiles; they will even eat small fish, as well as the eggs and young of other birds. They frequent farms, towns, and marshy areas. Their song, which sounds like a rusty gate, is not particularly musical.

During courtship the male flattens its body toward the ground, moving slowly and emitting a strange squeaky squeal.

Scientists have found that a weak solution of ammonia water sprayed at night after the birds have settled in to roost is useful in repelling these winged pests. Grackles have, nevertheless, proven to be quite adaptable. Their numbers have increased dramatically since the days when most of the eastern parts of this country were still considered a forest wilderness.

The name grackle comes from the Latin word *graculus,* which describes a diverse group of black birds.

EARED GREBE

COMMON NAME: Grebe, Eared

SCIENTIFIC NAME: *Podiceps nigricollis*

DESCRIPTION: Measuring about 13 inches in length, this gregarious, ducklike water bird is dark all over except for delicate golden feathers that fan out from a conspicuously red eye. The neck is thin; the black head shows a crest in breeding plumage. The rump is held above the water. The horned grebe is slightly larger, usually about 14 inches long. It has a dark rufous chest and sides, and the head resembles a black hat with a yellow stripe fanning out from above the eye. In winter the eared grebe shows white below and dark above, with a dark cap. The smallest of North American grebes, the least grebe, is only 9 inches long and is dark gray with fluffy white undertail coverts. In winter its chin and throat are white.

HABITAT AND RANGE: Eared grebes live in the western parts of North America from Alaska, the Yukon, and the Northwest Territories through western United States and south to Mexico. They winter from central Texas west to the Pacific Coast. These birds prefer slow-moving streams as well as marshes, ponds, and lakes. During the winter, and in migration, they can also be seen in saltwater areas, such as bays, seacoasts, and estuaries. The horned grebe is found from Alaska and northern Canada south to Wisconsin. The least grebe is a southern species and lives in southern Texas south to South America.

Eared grebes are very social birds, nesting in colonies of as many as 100 birds. The colonies of this species are often so crowded that nests sometimes touch each other. In winter the flocks may include as many as 750,000 birds. Grebes are found throughout the world, making it difficult to determine their point of origin.

These birds are particularly sensitive to pollution. Lakes and ponds that have been polluted with detergents are deadly to these birds. Their plumage becomes waterlogged, and the birds, unable to float on the surface, drown. In cases where scientists and conservationists have caught and cleaned some of the affected birds, they recovered within two weeks.

Grebes are physiologically adapted for life on the water. They have short wings and unusual lobed toes and flattened claws that make swimming and diving effortless. Not surprisingly, however, these same characteristics make the grebes look a bit awkward on land, and they rarely fly.

Grebes possess the unusual ability to reduce their buoyancy and sink below the surface by squeezing the air from their plumage. This allows them to disappear and swim long distances underwater. This peculiar characteristic earned them some colorful common names during colonial times, including water witch and hell diver.

Both the genus and family name come from Latin words meaning "rump-footed" and refer to the location of the legs, close to the rear of the body. The name grebe probably came from the old English word *krib,* meaning "crest," a reference to the great crested grebe found in Europe.

The appearance of the grebe is explained in an old Native American legend. Manabush, an evil mythical figure, once brought all the birds together and marked some of them for death. The small grebe was one of these. Because he was so awkward on land, he could not run very fast and was quickly caught.

Manabush held him up with contempt and said that he wasn't worth killing, but that he would ever after have a red eye and all the birds would laugh at him. And with that he kicked him into Lake Michigan, and in the process, knocked off his tail. That is why today the little grebe has a bright red eye and almost no tail.

The nest of the grebe, which is made of iris leaves and other water weeds, floats, giving it extra protection in case of flooding. The grebe actually eats the feathers and down from its own chicks. It is believed that this helps to insulate its stomach and protect it from the sharp fish bones it ingests.

COMMON NAME: Grosbeak, Evening
SCIENTIFIC NAME: *Coccothraustes vespertinus*

DESCRIPTION: This stocky bird, measuring only 8 inches long, has a large, conical, seed-crushing bill and a dark yellow body fading to olive-brown on the head and throat. Distinctive bright yellow patches are found on the forehead and eyebrows. The black wings and tail show large white patches. The female is drab gray with just a hint of yellow.

HABITAT AND RANGE: The evening grosbeak inhabits spruce and fir forests and mixed deciduous woods from British Columbia south to New England and Minnesota.

The former genus name, *Hesperiphona,* derived from the Greek name for the evening star, Hesperus. Hesperides were daughters of night and lived on the western verges of the world. The latter part of the name, *-phona,* is from the Greek word *phone,* meaning "sound" or "voice"; thus the name was translated as "evening singer."

EVENING GROSBEAK

When the Europeans first came to the Americas, the natural range of the evening grosbeak did not extend any farther east than Minnesota. Perhaps due to the presence of suburban bird feeders, this species is now found in the New England states all the way to the Atlantic Ocean.

In winter the diet of these birds is made up of sunflower and other seeds found at bird feeders, and from the wild they eat the seeds of box elder, dogwood, maple, and wild cherry. Winter populations vary greatly in number from one year to the next. In spring, the outer covering of the beak of this bird peels off, exposing a lovely blue-green color underneath.

When first described by Major Delafield, a North American explorer of the early nineteenth century, evening grosbeaks were believed to hide in the shade during the day and come out only as the sun set, which is not an accurate description of their behavior, as they are active during daylight hours as well.

Evening grosbeaks sometimes land on roadways during winter months to pick up pieces of grit and rock salt, which varies their diet and aids in digestion of seeds and berries.

COMMON NAME: Grouse, Ruffed
SCIENTIFIC NAME: *Bonasa umbellus*

DESCRIPTION: This chicken-like bird has a fan-shaped tail with a dark band at the tip and is usually about 17 inches long. During courtship, the male will fan the tail to attract females. The body is finely barred with soft brown; the breast is light gray.

HABITAT AND RANGE: Ruffed grouse are spotted most frequently in heavy forests of both deciduous and coniferous trees, as well as in clearings in those woods. They usually winter among conifers. Their range extends from central Alaska southward to the northern edge of California, from northern Utah east to the Great Lakes area, and on to the Atlantic Coast and south through the Appalachians.

The voice of the ruffed grouse is a shy murmur, only used when the hen clucks to her chicks or when two adults are close to one another. A much louder noise is created by the males as they court the females. At this time they make a surprisingly loud drumming noise by beating the air with extremely rapid wing strokes. People used to

RUFFED GROUSE

believe that the male ruffed grouse made this noise by beating his wings against a hollow fallen log. John James Audubon described this sound as "a tremor in the air not unlike distant thunder."

The genus name *Bonasa* is from the Greek and Latin word *bonasus*, meaning "wild bull." This name was given to the grouse because the drumming sound the males make reminds one of the bellowing of a bull. The species name, *umbellus*, is from the same root word as that for "umbrella" and refers to the ruff of feathers on the side of the neck. The common name ruffed also refers to these feathers.

In winter the ruffed grouse grows tiny horny fringes on its toes that act as snowshoes—they spread out the bird's weight over the snow to keep it from sinking. During the cold months the bird feeds on catkins, buds, and the twigs of trees, particularly aspen and poplar.

The Ojibway Indians have a legend about why the grouse has spots on its tail. They explain that the eleven spots on a grouse's tail are left over from the time that the grouse would not do as it was told and had to fast eleven days as punishment.

A story is told by the Paiutes of the sage grouse. At one time most of the world was under water except for the very tip of a mountain, and there the last remnant of fire in the whole universe burned bravely. The Paiutes that lived through the great storms and flooding knew that their only hope of salvation was to get to the fire on top of this mountain. But the storms still raged and waves of water came close to putting out the fire. Finally a little sage grouse flew to the tip of the mountain and sat close to the fire, fanning it to keep it alive and protecting it from the drenching waves of the flood. Although she saved the fire, she paid dearly for her efforts. She sat so close to the flame that it scorched her breast, and to this day she carries a black breast to remind everyone of her heroism.

The Cherokee Indians considered the meat of ruffed grouse taboo for a pregnant woman. They considered it bad luck because although this bird lays a large number of eggs, few of them hatch and make it to maturity. In some Native American cultures, this meat was forbidden women until they were past the childbearing age.

The ruffed grouse is the state bird of Pennsylvania.

COMMON NAME: Gull, Bonaparte's

SCIENTIFIC NAME: *Larus philadelphia*

OTHER SPECIES: Laughing gull (*Larus atricilla*) and herring gull (*Larus argentatus*)

DESCRIPTION: During the winter breeding period, this small, black-hooded gull with a fan of white at the wing tip has red legs and a small black bill. It is approximately 13 inches long. Its graceful, ternlike flight with the bill held down makes it easy to identify.

A similar species is the laughing gull, which is about 16 inches long and has a black hood and dark gray mantle. The trailing edge of its wing has a narrow white band. In winter the head is grayish white.

The Herring gull is much larger, almost 25 inches long. It has a white head with gray mantle and a white tail. The wings are tipped with black and show two circular white spots.

HABITAT AND RANGE: Bonaparte's gull breeds on lakes and rivers where forests are abundant in Canada, and winters near estuaries along the Pacific Coast from Baja California to Canada and on the Atlantic coast south from New England to Florida and the Gulf Coast.

The laughing gull prefers saltwater coasts, including the southern part of California, the Gulf of Mexico, and around the coast of Florida and up to Long Island, sometimes as far north as the coastal provinces of Canada.

While breeding, the herring gull is found in central and eastern Alaska and across the northern provinces of Canada. After raising a family, it wanders widely, crisscrossing Canada and the United States.

Gulls, which are opportunistic feeders, are found abundantly along the coast, often feeding in garbage dumps and refuse heaps. They will carry clams and mussels in their beaks to a considerable height and then drop the mollusks onto hard-packed sand or a roadway to crack their shells. They nest near lakes, rivers, seacoasts, and bays, on tundra, islands, rocky shores, and cliffs.

In spite of the popularity of *Jonathan Livingston Seagull,* a sweet story written by Richard Bach about a gull in search of happiness, there is really no such thing as a "sea gull." Although many kinds of gulls are found in coastal areas, the term sea gull is a catch-all for many different species of gulls. Perhaps the species most often called a sea gull is the herring gull.

There are over forty-four different species of gulls found throughout the world, from the Arctic to Antarctica.

The name gull comes from the Welsh word, *gwylan,* meaning "wailing," from the

LAUGHING GULL

plaintive cry of these birds. This name goes back to the fourteenth century. The old Anglo-Saxon name was *meu,* a reference to its mewing cry.

The name laughing gull came from the voice of this bird, which is like a low chuckling laugh—"ha-ha-ha-ha-haah-haah." The Bonaparte gull was named for Charles-Lucien-Jules-Laurent Bonaparte, a nephew of the emperor, one of Europe's and America's finest ornithologists. Born in 1803, he was the eldest son of the emperor's brother. The genus name, *Larus,* is from a Latin word that translates as "ravenous seabird."

Before 1900, gull eggs were considered quite a delicacy. Country folk would go out collecting the eggs almost daily. After 1900, laws were enacted to protect the gull that banned the collection after the fourth of July. Eventually even stricter laws were passed, prohibiting the collection of gull eggs altogether.

Indian tribes from the northwestern parts of this country tell the story of a giant who had some oolachans (salmon-like fish) and cooked them over an open fire. The gulls came and ate the oolachans and the giant became so angry he threw the gulls into the fire where they burned their wings. And so the edges of a gull's wings are black today.

RED-TAILED HAWK

COMMON NAME: Hawk, Red-tailed
SCIENTIFIC NAME: *Buteo jamaicensis*

DESCRIPTION: A rather large, heavy bodied bird, the red-tailed hawk measures about 18 to 24 inches long and has a wide wingspread and a characteristic reddish tail. The plumage of this bird is variable, with two common phases—light and dark. During the light stage, the bird is uniformly whitish below, with a wash of brown color at the waistband. The dark stage is dark brown with a reddish cast across upper wings, chest, and belly. The coloration of males and females is similar.

HABITAT AND RANGE: Probably our most common hawk, this species is found throughout Canada and the United States, including Alaska. It is often seen perched on high-tension wires, poles, and fence posts. It frequents open woodlands, fields, and mountain areas as it searches for rodents, rabbits, the occasional small bird, and even grasshoppers.

One of the oldest of all recorded fables was told by Hesiod, a Greek poet of the eighth century B.C. A hawk catches a nightingale and prepares to eat him. The nightingale argues with the hawk, saying he is too small and insignificant to satisfy the mighty hawk, and pleads with him to release him. The hawk replies that a small bird who calms a little hunger is better than a big bird not yet caught.

Today's counterpart to this? "A bird in the hand is worth two in the bush."

This saying has many variations in different languages. The Scottish saying is "Better a fowl in the hand nor two flying"; the Hebrew: "One bird in the net is better than a hundred flying." The French tradition gives us "Better one `I have' than two `I shall haves'"; and the Germans say "A sparrow in the hand is better than a pheasant that flieth by."

The name hawk is from the Teutonic root *hab,* meaning "to seize or take hold." This, of course, refers to the terrific grasping power of these birds of prey. The family name also refers to this characteristic: the designation Accipitridae is from the Latin word *accipere,* meaning "to take or seize."

In Iceland it was believed that if a person carried a hawk's tongue underneath his own tongue he would understand the language of birds.

The following is a story told by a medicine man of the Pomo Indians of California about how light came into the world:

The world was in darkness, and one day the coyote and the hawk bumped into each other. They commiserated on how awful the darkness was and set about thinking how they could make light. The coyote made a huge ball of stalks from bulrushes he had gathered.

He gave this and some pieces of flint to the hawk, who flew with them, higher and higher. He rubbed the flints and sparked the bundle of rushes ablaze, and it burned with light and heat. That is how the sun was created. The coyote made another ball of rushes and this time used damp reeds. Again the hawk flew up and lighted it, but it hardly burned, only putting out a pale, silver smoke—this was the moon.

During courtship a pair of hawks will fly close together, the male above, or he may spiral high above her and then drop in a spectacular swooping dive, which she meets, momentarily locking talons with him.

How the wings and tail of a bird are built dictates not only what it preys upon but also its habitat. Falcons have long, graceful wings for power and speed. These are perfect for the wide open spaces where it is found. The wings of Accipters—hawks with short wings and long tails—are beautifully adapted to the many twists and turns necessary to chase prey through scrub and woodlands, the natural habitat for many different kinds of hawks.

Although hawks do not appear in as many tales and legends as eagles do, a few do mention the hawk. Zora Neale Hurston relates the following tale about the hawk in her book *Mules and Men*:

A young hawk and an old buzzard were stting in a pine tree. The hawk asked the buzzard how he made a living. The buzzard answered him that he made out pretty well just waiting on the salvation of the Lord. The hawk ruffled up his feathers and said that he didn't wait on the mercy of anyone. He looked after himself. The buzzard shook his head, "I bet I live to pick your bones," he told the hawk.

The hawk ignored him and flew to a nearby tree where a small sparrow was sitting on a dead branch. In his haste to catch his prey the hawk missed the sparrow but managed to pierce himself on the end of the sharp branch. He was stuck there and got weaker and weaker. Finally the buzzard flew by slowly, shaking his head. "I told you," he said, "I'll be here to pick your bones."

COMMON NAME: Heron, Great Blue
SCIENTIFIC NAME: *Ardea herodias*

DESCRIPTION: A large, slim, blue-gray wading bird that measures 39 to 52 inches long, the great blue heron is white about the head and throat and has a long, pointed, yellowish beak. Black plumes trail from behind the eyes to several inches away from the head. It stalks slowly through shallow water, head hunched on its shoulders. In flight the legs trail out from the body at full length, but the head is "pulled in" (drawn back to the shoulders). The male and the female have a similar appearance.

GREAT BLUE HERON

HABITAT AND RANGE: The great blue heron can be seen in tidal flats, along shorelines, and in salt and freshwater marshes coast to coast in central Canada, most of the United States, and a large portion of Mexico. This bird feeds on crawfish, frogs, and other aquatic life. On land it will sometimes take mice and insects.

In the tomb of Ti of the Old Kingdom of Egypt (2400 B.C.) kingfishers and herons are shown in a limestone relief of a hippopotamus hunt. In a slightly different art form, a great white heron was pictured on a U.S. postage stamp announcing the establishment of Everglades National Park.

Sometimes birds will learn new methods of acquiring food. The green-backed heron, which has developed some fairly sophisticated fishing methods, is a good example of this. It has been observed dropping small pieces of bread into the water to attract minnows, which it then eats.

Herons lack the oil glands that are so prominent in other kinds of water birds. Instead, they produce what is called "powder down," soft, downlike feathers that grow on the breast. As the barbs for these break down, they produce a powder-like substance that serves as insulation and waterproofing.

The Goliath heron lives in Africa and is nearly as tall as a man. To reduce competition for food, this long-legged giant wades out into the deep waters of lakes to get fish larger than other birds can handle.

The small black heron has a different feeding method altogether. It wades near the shore, runs a short distance and then freezes, wings outspread like an umbrella. It stands motionless in this position until a minnow swims into its shadow. The heron quickly snatches and eats the minnow, and then duplicates the procedure. It is not known if the minnows swim into the temporary shade supplied by the heron-umbrella or if the heron can simply see into the water better while it is blocking the sun.

The name heron is related, if distantly, to the Greek word *krizein,* "to cry out or shriek." The oldest heron ever recorded lived over 23 years.

COMMON NAME: Hummingbird, Ruby-throated

SCIENTIFIC NAME: *Archilochus colubris*

OTHER SPECIES: Anna's hummingbird (*Calypte anna*) and rufous hummingbird (*Selasphorus rufus*)

DESCRIPTION: The ruby-throated hummingbird measures only 3 inches long. The male has an iridescent scarlet throat patch, whitish gray belly and flanks, green back and crown, and a grayish black forked tail. The female is similar, but lacks the bright breast and its tail is rounded, with white spots.

HABITAT AND RANGE: This species is found in meadows, open forests, in gardens, or wherever there are flowers. This is the only hummingbird found east of the Mississippi River, except for an occasional stray. The breeding range extends throughout eastern Canada and the eastern half of the United States. In winter it migrates south across the Gulf of Mexico into Central America.

There are many species of hummingbirds found in the western United States. These include Anna's hummingbird, which is the only red-crowned hummingbird found in this country. The head and throat of the male is a brilliant crimson red; the underparts are grayish, the back green, and the tail slightly forked. The female lacks the red head and gorget (throat patch) and shows scattered red feathers on the throat. This species resides in California and Baja California, occasionally wandering inland to Arizona and along the Rockies north into Canada.

The rufous hummingbird is only 3 1/2 inches long. The male is the only North American hummingbird with a rufous (reddish) back. Its gorget in the male is an iridescent orangy-red, its breast white with buff-red underparts. The rufous's tail has dark tipped spots. The female is green-backed with no gorget. The rufous ranges farther north than any other hummingbird. It breeds as far north as southern Alaska. During migration it reaches Saskatchewan and Manitoba, then flies south through the Dakotas and down to Texas, wintering in Mexico. It prefers conifer forests, scrubby areas, and meadows.

B ecause of its brilliant plumage and tiny size, the little hummingbird has figured prominently in myths and legends. All of these stories are from the Americas, for this is the only natural range for the hummers. The sight of this diminutive bird must have been thrilling for the early explorers. In his journal entry of October 21, 1492, Christopher Columbus mentions "little birds . . . so different from ours it is a marvel," undoubtedly alluding to the tiny hummingbird.

Huitzilopochtli, whose name means "hummingbird of the south," was an Aztec god of sun and war. It was believed that Aztec

RUBY-THROATED HUMMINGBIRD

soldiers were reincarnated as hummingbirds. This bird was believed to be one of the original creators of the Universe.

A favorite myth of the Arawak Indians of Venezuela tells how their ancestors obtained the first tobacco plants from Trinidad by sending a hummingbird perched on the back of a crane to snatch and bring back the jealously guarded seeds.

In one Mayan legend, birds who asked a tribal wise man how to build a sturdy nest were sent to the hummingbirds for lessons.

In another legend of the Maya, the Great God was busy making different kinds of birds for the world. When he was finished, he found a tiny pile of scraps left over, and not wanting to waste them, decided to make the tiniest bird of all. He made a pair of hummingbirds and called all the birds together to celebrate. Many birds brought gifts for the couple. The house finch gave red feathers for a scarf for the hummingbird groom, who gave one or two to his wife. The sun, wanting to give a present too, shone down on the couple to make their feathers gleam and sparkle like gold and jewels. Since that time, the feathers of the hummingbird have been iridescent in the sunlight.

In a Navajo legend, the first hummingbird was big and white and always hungry. In its search for food it destroyed many flowers. The Great Spirit looked down on the hummingbird, displeased that it cared so little for the flowers, and decided to punish this large, awkward bird by shrinking its size so it would need less food. And so the hummingbird got smaller and smaller, and in the process, its vocal cords became small and twisted and soon it lost its song. The hummingbird was very sad. Not only was it small, it had no song! The other birds felt sorry for the hummingbird and asked the Great Spirit if it could be given colorful feathers to make up for the loss of its size and song. The Great Spirit agreed, and the hummingbird now has glorious feathers.

The Indian tribes of the American Southwest considered hummingbirds to be bringers of rain. They felt that the little hummer had a direct connection to the god of rain and could bring much-needed water to this region. Often water jars were decorated with stylized pictures of hummers. Hopi and Zuni tribes include the hummingbird in their ceremonial rain dances.

Although popular myth maintains that hummmingbirds must "hitchhike" on the back of a goose while migrating across the Gulf of Mexico, this is only a fairy tale. The little hummers eat well and rest before flying across the Gulf, which they do all on their own.

The hummingbird is a master of flight. It can hover over a flower and can fly forward and backward, up and down.

The genus name *Archilochus* is from the Greek for "chief brigand," perhaps referring to the outstanding plumage of these birds. The genus, *Selasphorus,* is from the Greek word for "light-bearing," an illusion to the bird's brightly colored feathers.

Anna's hummingbird is named for Anna de Belle Massena (1806–1896), a woman described by Audubon as a "beautiful young woman, not more than twenty, extremely graceful and polite."

The wings of the broad-tailed hummingbird beat fifty to seventy-five times a second. This rapid beat of wings creates the unmistakable humming sound that gives this tiny bird its common name. The ruby-throated hummingbird has the highest metabolic rate of any warm-blooded vertebrate in the world.

Hummingbirds will aggressively protect their food source, even when they are satiated. This is why hummingbirds appear to fuss and argue around a feeder. In addition to nectar, hummingbirds will eat beetles, ants, aphids, and gnats.

Most hummingbirds are not even as long as a bald eagle's middle toe.

BLUE JAY

COMMON NAME: Jay, Blue

SCIENTIFIC NAME: *Cyanocitta cristata*

DESCRIPTION: This noisy and fearless, crested, blue-backed jay measures 12 inches long and has white spots on its wings and at the tip of its tail. Its underparts are grayish. The throat is white, decorated with a black band resembling a necklace. The male and the female look alike.

HABITAT AND RANGE: Blue jays are found most often at the edges of deciduous-coniferous forests (oak and pine) and in residential areas. They are found throughout the eastern United States and Canada, but their range is extending westward. By 1990, blue jays were common in Alberta and British Columbia. Wandering or migratory blue jays have been spotted in several western states.

Incessantly noisy and omnivorous, the gregarious blue jay is difficult to ignore. It makes its presence known with its flashy plumage and loud cries. These birds seem to eat everything from fruits and nuts to the eggs and nestlings of other birds.

The name jay may have come from the Latin nickname "*Gaius,*" meaning "gay, merry." The species name *cristata* derives from the Latin word *crista,* meaning "crested."

Jays are very tame around humans. Although they usually have a shrill and raucous cry, they can also emit a soft, low song. An admirable mimic, the blue jay can make a sound that is amazingly like the cry of the red-shouldered hawk.

Southerners say that the blue jay was yoked to a plow by a sparrow. The mark left by the yoke can still be seen on the blue jay's breast.

The Cherokee Indians suggest that if you find a blue jay's feather, soak it in water, and then gently brush a child's eye with it, the child will become an early riser. This will not work if the feather is taken from the bird; it must be found on the ground.

Indians from the Hudson Bay area believed that the Canada jay cried out a warning whenever they tried to sneak up on an Eskimo camp. For this reason, the Indians often killed the Canada jay.

Because blue jays do not always retrieve all of the acorns and other seeds they bury in the fall, they are friends to the forest by "planting" new seeds.

DARK-EYED JUNCO

COMMON NAME: Junco, Dark-eyed
SCIENTIFIC NAME: *Junco hyemalis*

DESCRIPTION: Measuring only 6 inches long, the dark eyed junco appears in such diverse forms that until 1983 this bird was listed as four separate species: white-winged junco, slate-colored junco, gray-headed junco, and Oregon junco. The Committee on Classification and Nomenclature of the American Ornithologists' Union (AOU) decided to lump them into one complex species: the dark-eyed junco. This bird has a dark hood, a grayish white belly, and sometimes buff-pink sides. The Oregon junco has a rufous back, delft blue-gray head, tail, and wings, and a black hood. When the junco flys away, two white outer tail feathers show conspicuously.

HABITAT AND RANGE: These birds prefer open coniferous and deciduous forests. They can also be seen in brushy clearings, bogs and roadsides. They are attracted to suburban areas with feeders. Their range includes Alaska, Canada, and almost all of the United States.

Juncos usually winter in the same area year after year. At feeders, which they frequent, the birdwatcher can observe a definite hierarchy. Juncos of greater stature will chase off less important juncos, effectively establishing the pecking order. Males are usually at the top of the order, followed first by females, then by immature birds.

The name junco comes from the Latin word for "rush," a plant found in marshy areas, even though this species prefers open pine woodlands. The name *hyemalis* is Latin for "wintry." It was often thought that juncos are called "snowbirds" because their arrival foretells the coming of winter to their southern range. Another possible source for the nickname snowbird may be the white belly of the slate-colored junco, which has been described as "leaden skies above, snow below."

AMERICAN KESTREL

COMMON NAME: **Kestrel, American**

SCIENTIFIC NAME: *Falco sparverius*

DESCRIPTION: Formerly called sparrow hawk, the American kestrel measures about 9 to 12 inches in length. It is the only small hawk with a rufous-orange back and tail. The male has grayish blue wings; the female is less colorful, with rufous, dark-tipped wings. The face pattern is distinctive, having two black "sideburns" on each side of the head. The kestrel has a long barred tail with a black band at the tip. Wings are pointed and give a "bent-elbow" appearance.

HABITAT AND RANGE: American kestrels hunt from treetops and utility poles. They prefer open grasslands and semi-open country from cultivated lands to urban areas. They breed from central Alaska across Canada and south into the western United States, wintering throughout the south and central United States.

The American kestrel is a beautiful, though small, bird of prey. It does not dive and swoop for its prey like other predatory birds but hovers like a helicopter. Kestrels can even be seen doing this over highway medians. To remain in the same spot the kestrel beats its wing feathers rapidly, but even in a strong wind, its head will remain motionless. The Eurasian, or Old World, kestrel is sometimes called windhover.

The kestrel was at one time called the sparrow hawk. This is something of a misnomer, however, since only 15 percent of its diet is made up of small birds. Eighty percent of the kestrel's diet is composed of small rodents. It has been found that the kestrel can eat as many as 290 mice in a single year.

Like all birds of prey, the kestrel has uncommonly good eyesight, well suited to daytime vision. With eyes that are eight times better suited than a human's for detecting and tracking prey, a kestrel can spot a beetle from over 100 feet away.

Although kestrels prefer living in grasslands, they do need trees to nest in. If threatened while sitting in the nest, the kestrel will lie on its back and defend itself with its razor-like talons.

The species name *sparverius* is from the Latin word meaning "relating to a sparrow" and refers to both its size and to its sometime prey.

The common name kestrel may have been from the Latin word *crepitare*, meaning "to rattle or crackle," which describes the kind of call emitted by the kestrel.

KILLDEER

COMMON NAME: Killdeer

SCIENTIFIC NAME: *Charadrius vociferus*

DESCRIPTION: This 9- to 10-inch-long, ground-nesting plover has spotted eggs that blend in well with rocks and stones. The birds have a brown head and back and a rufous-orange rump, which is visible as it takes flight. From the front, two prominent black bands are conspicuous against a white throat and breast.

HABITAT AND RANGE: Killdeers prefer lakeshores, fields, meadows, airports, and mud flats. They breed in open, dry, or gravelly places. Their range covers Canada, the United States, Mexico, and sometimes even Alaska. They winter at lower altitudes where they can find ice-free ponds.

Killdeers illustrate very well a kind of camouflage known as disruptive coloration. The birds have a pure white breast crossed by two brown bands. Just like a zebra's stripes, these bands help the bird blend into the grasses of pastures and fields where it lives.

These birds are famous for their "broken wing" display. If a predator approaches the nest, the adult bird will flap its wings, fan its tail out toward the attacker, and make a big show of struggling away from the nest. The predator is induced to believe that the bird is injured and would be easy prey, and thus will be drawn away from the nest. Once the nest or young are out of danger, the killdeer undergoes a miraculous recovery and screams loudly at the intruder as it takes wing. Killdeer are also known to defend their nests even against such large animals as deer or cattle. They are aggressively protective of their nest and young.

Killdeer hatchlings are capable of fending for themselves almost immediately. Sometimes even within an hour the young birds can run and feed themselves. The reason for this is that the killdeer egg is very large relative to the size of the parent bird; it also undergoes a long incubation period, usually twenty-four to twenty-eight days.

The common name killdeer is imitative of its whistling call, which actually sounds more like "kill-deeh." It in no way suggests possible predatory inclinations of this small bird. The species name *vociferus* is from two Latin words, *vox,* meaning "voice," and *ferare,* "to bear"; it refers to the persistence of this bird's shrill cry.

EASTERN KINGBIRD

COMMON NAME: Kingbird, Eastern

SCIENTIFIC NAME: *Tyrranus tyrranus*

DESCRIPTION: With dark gray head, back, wings, and tail, kingbirds measure about 8 inches long. They have a white breast and underparts and show a white band across the tip of the tail.

HABITAT AND RANGE: Kingbirds prefer woods, farms, and suburban areas in central Canada south through most of the United States; they are rarely found in Alaska or California. The western kingbird, *Tyrannus verticalis,* often builds its nest on utility pole crossarms.

In spite of its small size, this bird has a bold and courageous demeanor. This was not a view held by everyone, however. Benjamin Franklin, unhappy over the choice of the bald eagle as the national bird, wrote to his daughter Sarah in 1784 that the eagle was a "rank coward and that even the little kingbird attacks him boldly and drives him out of the district."

The American writer and zoologist Francis Hobart Herrick disputed this claim in his 1934 book *The American Eagle,* saying that the eagle "is never driven from the neighborhood by the little kingbird or by any other living being excepting a man armed with a gun. To be sure, the doughty kingbirds trail after him whenever he crosses their vigilantly guarded nesting preserves."

"Doughty" is perhaps an understatement of the character of the kingbird. This bird becomes absolutely belligerent when it feels its nest and young are threatened, attacking even much larger birds if danger approaches. Not only will the kingbird fly toward the intruder, crying shrilly, it will actually land on the backs of bigger birds, inflicting as much pain as possible so that the predator will not want to renew the fight.

This trait is probably behind the origin of tales about small birds riding on the backs of bigger birds.

The scientific names are appropriate as *tyrannos* is Greek for "lord" or "king." The common name kingbird further underscores the dominating character of this bird.

BELTED KINGFISHER

COMMON NAME: Kingfisher, Belted

SCIENTIFIC NAME: *Ceryle alcyon*

DESCRIPTION: The kingfisher is a solitary bird with a large crested head and a strong, dagger-like bill. With medium blue back, wings, tail, and head, this bird is about 13 inches long. A wide blue band runs across the male's white breast. Its throat is also white. The female is similar to the male in appearance but has a second rust-colored breast band. The belted kingfisher gives a rattling call as it flies upstream or moves from perch to perch.

HABITAT AND RANGE: Perching above streams, ponds, and rivers, the belted kingfisher searches the water for fish. This bird occurs in much of Alaska and Canada and all across the United States.

The kingfisher is found on every continent on earth and is the subject of much superstition and legend.

The European kingfisher was sometimes called a halcyon and was prominent in Greek mythology. Halcyone was the daughter of the god of the wind, Aeolus, and the wife of Ceyx. Ceyx was tragically drowned on his way to consult the oracle of Apollo, and Halcyone was so grief stricken that she drowned herself in the sea so that she could be near her husband. The gods took pity on this couple and changed them into a pair of kingfishers. Zeus declared that in their honor, the winds should not blow for seven days before and seven days after the winter solstice, December 21. This two week period coincided with the nesting period of the kingfishers, and from that time onward, this time is known as the halcyon days.

In the Mediterranean Sea area, the bird was thought to be able to calm the seas during its incubation period. An old saying of sailors is: "So long as kingfishers are sitting on their eggs, no storm or tempest will disturb the ocean."

Cherokee Indians tell the following tale about how the kingfisher got his bill:

The poor kingfisher wanted to be a water bird but had neither webbed feet nor a good bill for fishing. The animals felt so sorry for him that they held a council and decided to make him a long sharp spear with which to fish. They fastened it to the front of his mouth and the happy kingfisher flew to the top of a tree to watch for fish. When he saw one, he darted into the water and surfaced with a fish in his bill. Since then the kingfisher has been just that—king of all the fishers.

The kingfisher plays a role in one of

mankind's many fire-theft tales. The following story came from the Andaman Islands off the coast of Thailand:

When the first ancestors appeared on the earth, they had no fire. Bilika the creator had a pearl shell and a red stone that she would strike together to create the wonderful, magical fire. The people saw this and they wanted this magic that would keep them warm on the cold nights. One day Bilika fell asleep beside the flame. When she woke it was to find Sir Kingfisher stealing the fire. Furious, she threw the pearl shell at him and cut off his wings and

tail; but, undaunted, he dived into the water and carried his bit of fire to Bet-ra-kuku, where he passed it on to the bronze-winged dove, who gave it to the rest. After this the kingfisher was turned into a man.

Legend says that the kingfisher was the second bird Noah sent out to look for land. The foolish kingfisher flew high up in the sky (thus her blue back) but too close to the sun and scorched her breast. Noah was so irritated with her that he made her stay on the deck of the Ark and catch her food from the water.

COMMON NAME: Kinglet, Ruby-crowned
SCIENTIFIC NAME: *Regulus calendula*

DESCRIPTION: A tiny, 4-inch-long, olive-gray bird, the ruby-crowned kinglet is characterized by its broken white eye-ring. It also has a white wing bar and, directly below, a wider black wing bar. This bird has a small bill and a short tail. The male has a crimson crown patch that is visible only when the bird is excited. Kinglets are active birds, moving quickly among branches with much flicking of wings.

HABITAT AND RANGE: The little kinglet prefers coniferous and deciduous forests, open woodlands, brush, and scrub. Its breeding range extends from Alaska across Canada to the Atlantic Coast. These birds winter throughout the United States and south into Mexico.

Kinglets are helpful to man because of their appetite for destructive insects. In the Pacific Northwest, the golden-crowned kinglet helps keep the pear psylla in check.

The song of the kinglet is surprisingly loud, considering the small size of this bird.

The little kinglet makes a nest from moss bound together with cobwebs. There the

RUBY-CROWNED KINGLET

female lays five to ten eggs in a nest so small that sometimes the eggs lie on top of one another.

Both the ruby-crowned and the golden-crowned kinglet travel in large flocks along with creepers, nuthatches, and chickadees. These flocks scour the forest together looking for insects. Because the ruby-crowned kinglet is so tiny, it can feed at the very tips of branches, a location too precarious for heavier birds.

The genus name *Regulus* is a diminutive form of the Latin word *rex*, meaning "king." Likewise, the common name kinglet is the English diminutive of *king*. Both these names refer to the crownlike plumage of the male, which is displayed most often during courtship.

COMMON NAME: Kite, Mississippi
SCIENTIFIC NAME: *Ictinia mississippiensis*

DESCRIPTION: This is a graceful, soaring, falcon-shaped bird measuring 12 to 14 inches in length. It has a dark gray mantle, a white head, and a long black unbarred, notched tail. It feeds in flight on insects and also preys on rodents and reptiles.

HABITAT AND RANGE: Kites are found in coastal areas, wooded streams, and windbreaks in the southern United States near the Gulf of Mexico. It winters in Central and South America.

The name kite has been used since A.D. 975. It is from the Greek meaning "to quarrel" and indicates the aggressive nature of this bird. In England, a kite is considered someone who takes advantage of or preys on another. The light, sail-like toy flown on a string was named for this graceful bird of prey.

The genus name *Ictinia* is from the Latin word *elanus,* meaning "to press forward, harass, drive on," which refers to the feeding habits of the bird.

The kite has associations with early Egypt-ian history. According to legend, it was a kite that first brought the book of religious laws and customs to Thebes. In honor of this messenger, sacred scribes wore a red cap decorated with a kite feather.

Although many birds were eaten by ancient peoples, the Old Testament law was adamant that certain birds should not be taken. In Leviticus 11:13–14 it states: "And these are they which ye shall have in abomination among the fowls; they shall not be eaten, they are an abomination: the eagle, and

MISSISSIPPI KITE

the ossifrage, and the osprey, and the vulture, and the kite after his kind."

An old Gypsy proverb says that "A carrion kite will never be good luck."

The kite population in the United States has decreased dramatically over the past few decades. Perhaps most hard hit is the Everglades kite, *Rostrhamus sociabilis.* (As the species name here suggests, kites are especially gregarious—more so than most other birds of prey—and are often seen flying in flocks.) This bird feeds almost exclusively on a small snail found in shallow waters and swamps. As more and more swamps were drained for development, this snail began to disappear, and with it the Everglades kite. For a while scientists feared that it was on the road to extinction, but rescue efforts have paid off and the population is now slowly increasing.

COMMON NAME: Lark, Horned
SCIENTIFIC NAME: *Eremophila alpestris*

DESCRIPTION: The horned lark is about 7 inches long. The "horns" are actually black tufts of feathers that stick up from the head. The male has a brownish gray body, and a yellow face and crown with black sideburns. The breast is whitish yellow and has a black bib. The black tail is bordered by white outer feathers. The female's coloration is similar but duller.

HABITAT AND RANGE: The horned lark is found in several quite diverse habitats, from shorelines to the tundra, airports to alpine meadows. They are frequently seen near towns and on golf courses that have ponds. Their range is broad, extending from Alaska and Canada southward throughout the United States.

Larks are associated with many folk sayings. In some areas, "going to look for a lark's nest" means the same thing as "going to see a man about a dog" or "answering the call of nature"—or, more to the point, "going to the bathroom."

Children who might have considered collecting eggs from certain birds' nests were deterred by the following Scottish saying:

> *The laverock and the lintie,*
> *The robin and the wren;*
> *If ye harry their nests*
> *Ye'll never thrive again.*

Laverock is the Scottish name for the skylark.

HORNED LARK

The song of the skylark has inspired poets, musicians, and artists. Scottish poet James Hogg called it the "bird of the wilderness, blithesome and cumberless."

Perhaps the most beautiful tribute to this bird comes from Percy Bysshe Shelley in his poem "To a Skylark":

Hail to thee, blithe spirit!
Bird thou never wert,
That from heaven, or near it,
Pourest thy full heart
In profuse strains of unpremeditated art.

The family name Alaudidae is from Welsh words *al,* meaning "great," and *awd,* which means "song," and refers to the beautiful songs of members of this family. The genus name *Eremophila* is from the Greek for "solitude loving"; the species name *alpestris* refers to mountains where it breeds.

Baby horned larks have vivid colored mouth linings emphasized by black dots pointing the way down their throats, a sight that arouses frantic efforts by the parents to make sure their babies are fed.

The horned lark is considered philopatric, or faithful to the birthplace. Every year after migration, these birds return to the place of origin.

COMMON NAME: Loon, Common

SCIENTIFIC NAME: *Gavia immer*

DESCRIPTION: The loon is a large bird, measuring 28 to 36 inches in length. It has a blackish green head and a large, strong bill. When breeding, the birds have interesting black-and-white checkered patterns on the back and show a white throat. Their winter plumage is much duller in appearance. Loons are strong swimmers and divers and feed on fish and crustaceans.

HABITAT AND RANGE: Loons nest on large, conifer-edged lakes and tundra ponds, primarily in the north. Their range extends north from the coastal waters of Alaska and Canada (including both the Pacific and Atlantic coasts) and the northern United States to the Arctic Circle. They winter by the sea, on the Pacific Coast from Baja southward and on the Atlantic Coast around Florida and into the Gulf of Mexico.

The expression "crazy as a loon" probably originated with the strange, spooky laughing sound that the loon makes. This quivering song carries for long distances over water. In winter the loon seems to rest its voice and is usually silent.

Scientists have done detailed studies of the different songs and calls that loons make. They have discovered that the strange laughing call is usually given when the birds are alarmed.

The common name for this bird is from the Scandinavian word for "diving bird." Loons have lobed, or webbed, feet for diving to great depths and have been known to dive 240 feet or more and stay submerged for up to fifteen minutes. Penguins are the only birds that can dive deeper. The body of the loon is very heavy, which suits it well for diving, though not so well for travel on land. Its legs are located far back on the body, which aids it

in diving, but causes it to fall forward sometimes when trying to walk. Sometimes the loon will go for months without taking its feet out of the water.

The loon's ability to dive so deep and stay submerged for long periods of time led many cultures to believe that this bird was capable of magic. An Eskimo legend tells of a young boy who became blind and appealed to the loon for help. The loon took the boy to a lake where they dived into the water together. Three times they dived deep into the lake; the third time they stayed down so long the boy thought he would surely drown, but when they emerged, he could see once again.

According to a Delaware Indian legend, the loon led survivors to dry land after the Great Flood. In a Lenni-Lenape creation story, a loon brought a speck of mud to the surface of the lake that once covered the world, thus helping to make the first dry land.

COMMON LOON

Daniel G. Brinton wrote about it in his book *Myths of the New World*, published in 1868:

> *A loon flew that way, which they asked to dive and bring up land. He complied but found no bottom. Then he flew away and returned with a small quantity of earth in his bill. Guided by him, the turtle swam to a place where a spot of dry land was found. There the survivors settled and repeopled the land.*

Young loons can dive when they are only two days old. By the time they are a week old, they can dive up to 10 feet, and will continue to improve their diving and flying abilities until, at the age of two to three months, they will leave their parents.

During the first few weeks of life, however, the young often ride on the backs of their parents. This is to keep the babies safe, of course, but also to provide warmth. When the parents get tired of carrying the young, they simply submerge and allow the chick to float off.

Loons need a large territory. On a lake 100 acres or less, only one pair of loons will nest. Sometimes two or more pair will nest on much larger lakes.

Loon populations have lately decreased. Environmental hazards such as acid rain and coastal oil spills have taken their toll on this strange, mystical bird.

The loon is the state bird of Minnesota.

BLACK-BILLED MAGPIE

COMMON NAME: Magpie, Black-billed

SCIENTIFIC NAME: *Pica pica*

DESCRIPTION: A noisy, large black-and-white bird with an extremely long tail, magpies measure 20 to 22 inches long. The head, bill, upper back, throat, breast, and wings are all jet black. The sides, belly, and scapulars (upper wing, or shoulder) are white. The long tail is greenish black.

HABITAT AND RANGE: Magpies are sociable birds and are found on farms, rangeland, tree-lined stream banks, foothills, and open woodlands. Their range covers all of western North America.

The following story about magpies comes from the tales of the Arabian Nights: A woman who devoted herself to religion was keeper of the bath in the house of the king. One day the queen handed her a necklace of priceless jewels to keep safe while she bathed. The woman, in the midst of her prayers, laid the necklace on the rug while she continued to pray. Looking through the window, a magpie saw the bright necklace, seized it, and hid it in a cranny in the palace wall. When the queen asked for the necklace, the woman did not know what had happened to it. Believing that the woman had stolen the necklace, the king had the woman beaten and thrown in prison.

A few days later the king himself saw the wicked magpie flying across the courtyard with the necklace. He immediately pardoned the poor innocent woman and set her free.

The following poem tells the future for those who happen to see a flock of magpies. The number of birds one saw indicated what was soon to happen.

One for sorrow, two for mirth,
Three for a wedding, four for a birth.
Five for silver, six for gold,
Seven for a secret not to be told.
Eight for heaven, nine for hell,
And ten for the devil's own sel'.

If you didn't care for your fortune as the magpies told it, however, not all was lost. The way out of this was to spit three times over your shoulder while saying, "Devil, devil, I defy thee."

A native American tale tells why women talk more than men:

Long ago a Shasta Indian man fell in love with a woman in his tribe. One moonlit night he told her of his love and asked her to marry him. The Indian woman was so happy she wanted to share her news with all her friends. She told everyone in the tribe, and when there was no one else to tell, she went to the forest telling every creature.

The young man heard congratulations from everyone. Every member of the tribe seemed to know each word that he had spoken to his beloved. Finally, the man could stand it no longer and ran to the forest for some peace and quiet. But it was not to be so, for the creatures of the forest had also heard the news and teased and taunted him about his words of love. The magpie, the worst chatterer in the forest, was particularly vocal in its teasing. Finally, in desperation, the Indian man shouted, "A curse on you all—women and magpies. Every woman is a like a magpie. She cannot keep quiet!" And the Indian man ran away deep into the forest where no one knew him.

Although the man has never been heard from since, his curse still holds, and women and magpies happily spend their days chattering. That is why, the Shasta Indians will tell you, women talk more than men.

The common name magpie is from Meg, the nickname for Margaret, and *pie,* a French word imitative of the bird's call. The genus and species names also come from the French word *pie.*

COMMON NAME: **Martin, Purple**

SCIENTIFIC NAME: *Progne subis*

DESCRIPTION: Measuring 7 to 8 inches in length, the purple martin is the largest American swallow. They are a glossy, dark blue-black all over. The female has a light buff breast, a gray throat, and dark, blackish wings. The tail is decidedly forked.

HABITAT AND RANGE: These birds are found in the United States everywhere east of the Rockies as well as along the Pacific Coast. They prefer open areas, either rural or suburban.

Purple martins have an uncanny homing instinct. Scientists once took a martin from its nest in northern Michigan, put it in a car, and drove 234 miles south. The bird, which was released at night, showed up back in its nest the next morning, exactly eight hours and thirty-five minutes later.

Purple martins like to nest in groups, which is why the "apartment house" style of bird boxes make popular nesting spots for these birds. As many as 200 pairs sometimes breed together in very large houses.

Before wooden birdhouses came into vogue, gourds were hung up in a line to attract martins. A book on the history of the Carolinas suggests that pioneers put up gourd

PURPLE MARTIN

birdhouses as long ago as the 1700s. "The planters put gourds on standing poles on purpose for these fowl to build in, because they are a very warlike bird and beat the crows from the plantations." It is believed that the Indians used this technique even before the pioneers arrived.

Martin houses are still popular. Not only is it interesting to watch the nesting habits of these birds, but it is also useful to have populations of purple martins close to the house because these birds feed on many different insects, including mosquitoes. Although the martins do indeed eat mosquitoes, the claims of their being a good control for this are probably exaggerated. By the time the mosquitoes really come out in the evening most martins have already gone to roost.

Martins generally feed on flies, beetles, grasshoppers, and dragonflies, all of which are out in the heat of the day.

In the western United States, purple martins generally prefer to nest in holes left by woodpeckers in dead trees or in saguaro cacti.

The genus *Progne* is named for Procne, a daughter of King Pandion of Athens, whom the gods, according to Greek mythology, turned into a swallow. The purple martin, belonging to the family Hirundinidae, is considered a swallow.

COMMON NAME: Meadowlark, Western

SCIENTIFIC NAME: *Sturnella neglecta*

DESCRIPTION: A robin-sized, chunky field bird, the meadowlark measures about 9 inches in length. It has a tan-brown back, and a brownish short tail with white feathers on either side; these conspicuous white marks are best seen when the bird is flushed. The throat and belly are bright yellow, and there is a prominent black V mark on the yellow breast. It has white and brown stripes on its head. The western meadowlark is very similar to its eastern cousin in appearance, but their songs are quite different.

HABITAT AND RANGE: This bird is most often seen in plowed fields, pastures, meadows, and prairies—also near airports, and on the fences and posts surrounding them. It is found from the edge of the boreal forests in Canada (on the northern prairies of central Canada) south through the western states and into Mexico, and from the Pacific states east to the Mississippi River.

WESTERN MEADOWLARK

The eastern and western meadowlarks are so similar, it is difficult to tell them apart even when they stand side by side. The voices, however, are distinctly different. The song of the western meadowlark is described as being fluty and gurgley, and so musical that Hollywood often records it when they need a birdsong. The song of the eastern bird is said to be clear and high-pitched, sounding like "spring-of-the-year!"

The nest of both birds is created in a small depression in the ground and covered with a tightly woven grass dome. The nests are often found in hay fields, and are destroyed when the hay is harvested. The birds are usually able to build another nest and raise one more brood before the end of the season.

The genus name *Sturnella* is the diminutive form of the Latin *sturnus,* or "starling." *Neglecta* is from the Latin for "neglected or overlooked," as this species was because it so closely resembles the eastern meadowlark.

The western meadowlark is so well loved that six states have chosen it as their state bird: Kansas, Montana, Nebraska, North Dakota, Oregon, and Wyoming.

Both the eastern and western meadowlarks are polygynous and often more than one female and more than one nest will be found in one male's territory. The young of this species have white hairlike growths on the roofs of their mouths that point toward the throat for easy identification and feeding.

The Cherokee Indian name for the meadowlark is *nakwisi,* which means "star," and is descriptive of the shape of the tail as it spreads when the bird flies. A Cherokee legend tells of how the coyote changed himself into an elk and covered his body with a hard shell. The shell was not quite big enough to cover everything, however, and there was a small hole left at his throat.

The coyote was wicked as an elk, and killed people by tracking them down and stabbing them with his antlers. The people tried to defend themselves, but their arrows bounced off the hard shell of the elk. One day the little meadowlark sat watching the elk and suddenly cried to the hunters, "There is a hole at his throat!" Quickly a hunter shot an arrow from his bow and pierced the elk in the throat. Since that time the meadowlark has been beloved and held in high esteem.

COMMON NAME: **Merlin**
SCIENTIFIC NAME: *Falco columbarius*

DESCRIPTION: This small bird of prey measures about 12 inches in length. The male has a bluish back and a streaked and spotted brown head, neck, and breast. The face is plain brownish gray; the tail of the female is barred, with black and tannish stripes.

MERLIN

HABITAT AND RANGE: Merlins breed throughout Canada and Alaska. They winter in coastal areas of the United States, along the Mississippi River, and in the lower half of all the southern states. Their preferred habitats include wooded fields and open forests, tundra and marshes, and feedlots where there are pigeons. Merlins prey on shorebirds, mice, and insects.

The name merlin was primarily used by the British to describe this bird. Americans called it the pigeon hawk because it so often preys on pigeons. In 1973 the American Ornithologists' Union approved the change of name to merlin.

In the days of falconry, a merlin was the term used for the female bird. It has also been suggested that this name came from the old German word for "blackbird."

The species name *columbarius* is from a Latin noun meaning "pigeon keeper." This would seem to be something of a misnomer, since the merlin keeps pigeons only long enough to eat them. Small birds make up a large portion of the merlin's diet.

The nostrils of this bird are designed to allow free passage of air even when it is flying at great speeds. Merlins are adept at maneuvering in the air and using their strong talons to catch prey.

COMMON NAME: **Mockingbird, Northern**
SCIENTIFIC NAME: *Mimus polyglottos*

DESCRIPTION: The robin-sized mockingbird measures about 10 inches in length. It is a slim, gray bird, darker gray on the back with white outer tail feathers. The wings have white arches that are very noticeable in flight. Its song is remarkable for its wide repertoire. It can imitate other birds—even airplanes—and will often sing at night when there is bright moonlight.

HABITAT AND RANGE: Mockingbirds are found throughout the Southeast and the lower half of Texas, as well as in New Mexico, Arizona, and California. Their range seems to be expanding northward, and these birds have been spotted along the Atlantic Coast and sporadically in New England. They are seen most often in towns, farms, fencerows, shrubby areas, semi-desert, gardens, and urban areas.

NORTHERN MOCKINGBIRD

The mockingbird's song was considered so beautiful that great numbers of these birds were captured in the wild while young and kept as caged birds until laws were passed making the practice illegal. Its uncanny ability to mimic many different sounds (including crickets and frogs) is used by the mockingbird for more than just entertainment. Ornithologists have discovered that females are attracted to the males with the greatest vocal abilities—an added incentive for the males of the species to develop their vocabulary.

The song of the mockingbird has always fascinated those who are lucky enough to live near it. The Choctaw Indians called this bird *hushi balbaha,* meaning "the bird that speaks a foreign language."

The Cherokee Indians believed that the mockingbird, which they called *huhu,* had supernatural powers because it could imitate so easily. They would take the heart from this bird and give it to children to help them learn more quickly.

The Cherokees tell the following tale of the *huhu:* Once there was an old woman whose husband had died and who had a single daughter. She was always urging the daughter to get married so that they would have a man to help with the work. Finally a stranger came to their home and soon fell in love with the daughter. The mother asked if he worked hard and he assured her that he did. So she allowed him to marry her daughter.

The first day after the wedding, she gave her new son-in-law a hoe and told him to go down by the creek to work. All morning she heard the sound of a hoe hitting stone but when she went to find him at midday, she only found a small bit of ground had been worked. She listened carefully and heard the *huhus* (or mockingbirds) in the thicket.

The next day she sent him back to work, and again she heard the sound of the hoe against the stone. But when she crept up to the spot where he was supposed to be working, she found the hoe lying on the ground and the sounds of work coming from the thicket where only the *huhus* lived. The old woman realized that her new son-in-law was a mockingbird in disguise.

The Pueblo Indians believed that it was the mockingbird that gave the gift of speech to humans. A Texan-Mexican folktale relates how the mockingbird received the white markings on its wings. The story goes that at the beginning of time, all the animals spoke Spanish. But the mockingbird was so proud of his song he became conceited, declaring that it was he that caused the flowers to dance.

His mate, fearful of this newfound pride, added, ". . . *con el favor de Dios*" ("with the help of God"). But the mockingbird would not listen and the next morning began to sing to the flowers. Just as he began his song, a hawk snatched him up and carried him away. The frightened mockingbird cried out, "*Con el favor de Dios!*" admitting that he could do nothing without the help of the Lord. The hawk dropped him in a field, tearing his wings in the process. As he lay bleeding, a dove came to him and, taking white feathers from her own back, healed him. Since then, the mockingbird has worn these white feathers as a reminder to be humble.

William Bartram, the early Colonial nature lover, wrote of the mockingbird's song that it sounded like an attempt to "recover or recall his very soul, expired in the last elevated strain."

The mockingbird eventually became a symbol of the romantic image of the American South, and many well-known writers heaped praises on its small back. James Fenimore Cooper, Henry David Thoreau, and John Burroughs all wrote about this little bird with its big and exciting song.

It is perhaps Walt Whitman's poem "Out of the Cradle Endlessly Rocking" that brought the greatest literary attention to the mockingbird. It is from this poem that the mockingbird first began to become a symbol of hope.

In Harper Lee's novel *To Kill a Mockingbird,* published in 1960, the mockingbird is a symbol of the innocent and the helpless.

The genus name *mimus* is the Greek word for "mimic"; and *polyglottos* is Greek for "many-tongued."

The mockingbird will not hesitate to defend its territory, even against much larger and stronger birds. This characteristic was taken into consideration when Texas chose this bird as its state symbol in 1927. The Texas legislature's resolution says that the mockingbird is "a fighter for the protection of his home, falling, if need be, in its defense, like any true Texan . . . ."

COMMON NIGHTHAWK

COMMON NAME: Nighthawk, Common

SCIENTIFIC NAME: *Chordeiles minor*

DESCRIPTION: Measuring 8 to 10 inches in length, the nighthawk is mostly mottled brown with a white throat and a brown barred tail. A wide white band and a black band appear at the end of its notched tail. Seen overhead, it shows a wide white band halfway between "elbow" and tip of wing. This bird, as suggested by its name, hunts at night; during the day, it rests (perches) *horizontally* on tree limbs. It also sometimes rests on the ground, where it is easily camouflaged by the forest floor.

HABITAT AND RANGE: From northern Canada down to Mexico and from the Pacific to the Atlantic Coast, the nighthawk is seen in scattered pine woods and open country. It is often spotted high in the sky over cities and towns.

The nighthawk is not a hawk but a member of the nightjar family, which includes common nocturnal birds such as chuck-will's-widow and whippoorwill. It got its name because in flight it looks like a hawk. The nighthawk makes a buzzing noise that sounds like a large insect. This noise has given rise to other common names, such as pork-and-beans and bullbat. The bird's call is thought to sound like a nasal pronunciation of the word *"bean,"* or perhaps the sound that a bullfrog makes.

One or two eggs are laid by the female nighthawk, sometimes in such strange places as flat roofs of buildings in cities. More commonly, the eggs are laid on rocks or soil.

Nighthawks are known to be fantastic eaters, consuming great numbers of flying insects. Stomach analysis of captured birds has ascertained that nighthawks are capable of eating over 500 mosquitoes in a single day.

The family name, Caprimulgidae, is from the Latin word *capra,* meaning "goat," and *mulgus,* meaning "to milk." The name derives from the old belief that these birds used their wide mouths to obtain milk from mama goats. The genus *Chordeiles* is from the Greek word *chordelles,* meaning "evening traveler."

According to the Taos Indians, the nighthawk is a great hunter and legends tell of its returning from a hunt with a whole deer. The Zunis collected its feathers for prayer sticks, which they used in hunting and war ceremonies. They also used these feathers as offerings in newly turned fields, in the hopes that the field would catch the rain and runoff from nearby hills.

WHITE-BREASTED NUTHATCH

COMMON NAME: Nuthatch, White-breasted
SCIENTIFIC NAME: *Sitta carolinensis*

DESCRIPTION: This little forest bird is only 5 to 6 inches long. Its unique shape and feeding habits make it easy to identify. It is a small, compact bird tapered at both ends. It has a black cap, white face, throat, breast, sides, and belly, and a black eye on a white background. The bird's overall color is a blue-gray, and it has a short, narrow tail.

The nuthatch has a habit of searching along tree trunks for insects and larvae. The white-breasted nuthatch travels down the tree trunk head first, spiraling around the trunk as it probes for food, all the while softly saying "yank, yank, yank." The sexes are similar in appearance and voice.

HABITAT AND RANGE: Nuthatches are seen most often among deciduous trees, conifers, and piñon-juniper forests. They frequent feeders, particularly if found near shade trees. This bird is rarely seen on the Pacific Coast, but is scattered through all the western states and all across the southern and eastern states.

The name nuthatch is a corruption of "nuthack," which refers to the habit of this bird of securing a seed in a crack in a log and then hacking away at it with its beak until it opens.

Nuthatches characteristically scamper, unlike woodpeckers, which seem to hop up a trunk. The legs and feet of nuthatches are perfectly designed for balance and for catching on to bark and other rough surfaces.

The Cherokees call the nuthatch *tsuliena,* meaning "deaf," for the bird is so tame around humans it appears deaf to man-made noises.

Nuthatches will nest in boxes placed in trees or on the tops of tree trunks.

NORTHERN ORIOLE

COMMON NAME: Oriole, Northern
SCIENTIFIC NAME: *Icterus galbula*

DESCRIPTION: Orioles measure 7 to 8 inches long. There are two varieties of the northern oriole, the eastern and the western. In the eastern variety, formerly called the Baltimore oriole, the sexes look distinctly different. The male has a black head, throat, back, and wings and a brilliant orange breast; the female is olive-yellow above, yellow below. The western bird, also known as Bullock's oriole, differs from the eastern form in that it has orange cheeks and wide white wing patches; in the female the underparts are grayish white.

HABITAT AND RANGE: Orioles inhabit deciduous shade trees in suburban areas and scattered trees in open woodlands and orchards. They breed in the lower provinces of Canada, throughout the United States, and also into Mexico. The favorite nesting site is at the end of elm branches.

Though the eastern and western orioles occupy different ranges, they are actually one species and often interbreed in the midwest where their ranges overlap. In autumn the orioles migrate to tropical rainforest areas.

The genus name *Icterus* is from the Greek *ikteros*, meaning "jaundice," and refers to the myth that the sight of the oriole would cure jaundice. The species name *galbula* is from the Latin word for "small yellow bird."

To many Southwest Indian tribes, the yellow oriole represented yellow flowers and corn pollen.

The northern oriole was for many years called the Baltimore oriole. It was named for George Calvert (1580–1632), Baron of Baltimore, whose livery was bright yellow and black.

Among the most skillful of nestbuilders, the oriole carefully builds its nest of grass, twine, and weed fiber and then hangs it from the tips of the branches. The nest often includes bits and scraps of yarn and it is said countrywomen had to keep an eye on the weaving yarn they hung in the sun to bleach; otherwise the orioles would steal it away to put in their nests.

The major league baseball team that adopted this name also adopted the black and bright orange colors.

Orioles can be both helpful and harmful to crops that people grow. They have a voracious appetite for the cotton boll weevil but also like to eat blueberries, grapes, and other small fruits.

Edgar Fawcett, an American playwright and poet (1847–1904), wrote:

How falls it, oriole, thou hast come to fly
In tropic splendor through our Northern sky?
At some glad moment was it Nature's choice
To dower a scrap of sunset with a voice?

The northern oriole is the state bird of Maryland.

OSPREY

COMMON NAME: Osprey

SCIENTIFIC NAME: *Panidon haliaetus*

DESCRIPTION: This large bird measures 22 inches in length and is brownish black above and white below. When the bird is in flight and seen from below, black oval patches appear on the edge of the wing at the crook in the "elbow." Light tan and brown bars are on the tail, and the head is largely white, with dark cheek patches.

RANGE AND HABITAT: Ospreys breed from Alaska south to Florida and are found along coastal areas, rivers, streams, and lakes. Ospreys are found throughout the world in every temperate region except New Zealand and Hawaii.

Often called a "fish hawk," the osprey is well known for its method of catching fish. The osprey does not dive but plunges feet first to snatch prey from the surface or just beneath the water's surface. These birds sometimes fall from as high as 100 feet above the water. Their feet are highly adapted for capturing their prey and have sharp spines that help hold slippery fish.

Ospreys are so adept at catching fish that tales of magical powers were told about these birds by many Indian tribes. One of these stories says that the osprey has an oily substance on its body that is so enticing to fish that they are immediately drawn to it. If a piece of bait is touched with this oil, fish cannot resist it.

The genus name, *Panidon,* is from Pandion, king of Athens, whose daughters, Procne and Philomela, with their joint husband, Tereus, were transformed into birds. The species name *Haliaetus* is from the Greek word for "sea eagle."

The common name osprey is from the Latin *os,* meaning "bone," and *frangere,* "to break." This alludes to the belief that the birds have a habit of dropping bones from great heights to break them and use the fragments in their nest. These birds are sometimes called "short-toed eagles."

Shakespeare referred to the power of osprey in *Coriolanus:* "As is the osprey to the fish who takes it by sovereignty of nature."

Audubon described the courtship of the ospreys saying that

> *they sail by the side or after the female which they have selected, uttering cries of joy and exultation, alighting on the branches of the tree on which their last year's nest is yet seen remaining, and doubtless congratulating each other on finding their home again. Their caresses are mutual.*

The osprey nest is used year after year, the birds adding new material as needed. After many years these nests may become extremely large and cumbersome. Many strange items have been found in these nests, including shells, muskrat skulls, and plastic. Some of these nests have been used as long as forty years.

Unfortunately, the osprey population has been reduced as a result of hunting, as well as from their eating fish poisoned with pesticides, which causes them to lay infertile eggs. Fortunately, this situation is being reversed and there has been a slight population increase.

COMMON NAME: Owl, Great Horned

SCIENTIFIC NAME: *Bubo virginianus*

OTHER SPECIES: Snowy owl (*Nyetea scandiaca*) and screech owl (*Otus asio*)

DESCRIPTION: Measuring 18 to 24 inches long, this large owl has prominent ear tufts, which explains the common name, "horned." This bird has a very large head and appears to have no neck. There is a white patch on the throat, and the breast is brownish with horizontal barring.

HABITAT AND RANGE: These birds live in large trees in open country, wooded areas and stream sides throughout Alaska, Canada, the United States, and Mexico.

Other species of owls include the snowy owl, which is 24 inches long and all white. It has yellow eyes and no ear tufts. It lives in tundra areas and hunts during the daylight hours.

The eastern screech owl is much smaller, measuring only 9 inches. It goes through two distinct color phases and can be seen as all reddish brown or all gray. The ear tufts on this species are prominent and can be raised or flattened. White spots are found on the wings, and the tail is short. The range for this bird extends from the Rockies east to the Atlantic and south into Mexico. It is nocturnal.

Owls have been known and revered for many thousands of years. Humans have always had great respect for owls and have often considered them supernatural in their powers. One of the earliest drawings showing an owl dates back to the early Paleolithic period—a family of snowy owls was painted on a cave wall in the Dordogne region of France.

In the golden days of Greece, a small owl was found nesting in the cliffs near the Acropolis. Legend tells us that this little bird was instrumental in helping the Greeks win a big victory over the Persians: The owls gath-

GREAT HORNED OWL

ered in great flocks and then descended on the enemy, causing mass confusion and fear. Since that time the owl has been considered the mascot of Athens, and was even named for the goddess Athena. The scientific name of the bird is *Athene noctua*.

Another important deity, the Sumerian goddess of the underworld, Lilith, is usually depicted with wings and talons and is always accompanied by two owls. Lilith's name is translated in the Authorized Version of the Bible as "screech owl." A tablet showing a likeness of Lilith and her owls dates back to 2300–2000 B.C.

The belief that owls were wise originated in the days of King Arthur, when Merlin was always shown with an owl on his shoulder. During the Middle Ages the owl became an important symbol of learning and intelligence. Even today this myth persists, as evidenced by this anonymous nursery rhyme:

A wise old owl sat in an oak,
The more he saw the less he spoke,
The less he spoke, the more he heard,
Why can't we all be like that wise old bird?

Owls have also been considered harbingers of evil and doom for centuries. Pliny the Elder, a Roman statesman, wrote of the owl: ". . . when it appears [it] foretells nothing but evil, [and] is more to be dreaded than any other bird. . . ."

The Chinese believed that owls snatched away the soul, and whenever one heard the call of an owl, someone would say, "he's digging the grave." In many different cultures, to hear the call of the owl meant that death was coming. If the call was far away and muffled, death would come to someone close to you. If the call was clear and distinct, death would come to someone far away.

The Aztecs associated the owl with the

god of the dead and believed that anyone who hears the cry of the owl at night will die. In Italy this superstition takes on an unusual twist. If an owl is heard outside the home of someone sick, he was expected to die three days later. If heard outside a home where no one was ill, someone in the house would get tonsillitis.

In southern Australia many native tribes believe that bats looked after the lives of men, and owls were sacred to women. In some tribes it was believed that when the medicine men of the tribe died, their souls returned as owls. The owl, when he died, returned as a cricket.

Owls were also tellers of other news. In France if a pregnant woman heard the shriek of an owl, she knew she would have a girl. In Wales if a young woman heard an owl, she was sure to lose her virginity soon.

Owls were also thought to have the power to ward off evil. The Japanese put pictures and figures of owls on their houses in times of famine or epidemic in the hope that their home would be spared. Many North American Indian tribes believed that eating an owl's eye could help one see at night, or could restore lost eyesight. In Yorkshire, it was believed that owl soup would cure the whooping cough. An owl feather under the pillow was thought to make one sleep peacefully all night.

The owl turns up as a canny creature in Eskimo lore and is seen as a worthy antagonist to the sly coyote in the lore of the Zunis and other southwestern American Indians.

The Cherokee Indians tell the following myth about how the owl got its unusual markings:

When the world was first formed, there was no fire and all the creatures were cold. Then the Thunders sent Lightning and put fire in a hollow tree on an island. Although the animals saw the smoke, they could not cross the water to get the warmth. An animal council was held, and every animal that could swim or fly offered to help. The raven, with his strong wings and strong spirit was sent first. When he came close to the fire he became confused and landed on a tree limb to consider what to do next. As he sat there the fire scorched his wings so that they turned all black and he had to return without the fire. Next the screech owl tried but as he came close to the fire, he looked down into the hollow tree and a blast of hot air came up and burned his eyes. Even today his eyes remain red. Then the hooting owl and horned owl tried but the fire was so strong that the ashes blew into their eyes making white rings. These birds still carry the mark of the fire today.

Part of the owl's fascination for us lies in the fact that they are generally nocturnal, at home in the world of darkness that is so alien to us. Nocturnal owls hunt primarily with their ears.

AMERICAN WHITE PELICAN

COMMON NAME: Pelican, American White

SCIENTIFIC NAME: *Pelecanus erythrorhynchos*

OTHER SPECIES: Brown pelican (*Pelecanus occidentalis*)

DESCRIPTION: The familiar white pelican is a big water bird with a large yellow bill and black wings.

HABITAT AND RANGE: The pelican is transient throughout the West as well as the coastal regions of the Gulf and the lower Pacific Coast region. It feeds in shallow water by scooping up fish in its extendable bill as it swims on the surface of the water. It does not dive. Nests are found on West Coast or inland lakes.

The brown pelican is slightly smaller. The adult has a dark gray body and an all-white head and neck. During breeding season the back of the neck is rich brown.

The pelican is immediately recognizable by its prominent and capacious bill. One of the most popular verses about it says: "A wonderful bird, the pelican, / his bill can hold more than his belly can."

The species name *erythrorhynchos* is Greek for "red-beaked" and was given to this bird because its bill is reddish during breeding season.

Many poets and scholars have written about the pelican through the ages. A book entitled *The Anglo-Norman Bestiary* was written by Philip de Thaum in 1120. In it he suggests that young pelicans often died in the nest but were brought back to life when the mother would come and "pour her blood" over them. This superstition was held to be true for hundreds of years: Saint Jerome used the example of the mother pelican spilling her blood to save her children, just as Christ spilled his blood to save the world. Thus, the pelican has become a symbol of Christ and salvation.

It was believed that the pelican would actually peck at her own breast to give her young her life-saving blood. The expression "the pelican in its piety" probably dates to the thirteenth century, when Thomas Aquinas wrote a verse that began, "Pelican of Piety, Jesus, Lord and God. . . ."

Another early naturalist writer, Thomas Pennant, says in his book *Arctic Zoology* in 1784 that pelicans often fish together, "beating the water with their wings and feet in order to drive the fish into the centre." The pelicans were then believed to open their large mouths and fill them with fish that they would take to their young. Although pelicans do indeed fish together in this way, they do not use their large bills as carrying pouches.

The Seri Indian tribe from California attributed the creation of the world to the pelican, which they considered to be an ancient figure that at one time possessed supernatural wisdom and a beautiful song.

The pelican is thought to represent benevolent charity and parental love. Conversely, it is sometimes used as a symbol of dullness, indolence, and melancholy.

RING-NECKED PHEASANT

COMMON NAME: Pheasant, Ring-necked
SCIENTIFIC NAME: *Phasianus colchicus*

DESCRIPTION: This large, chicken-like bird has a long pointed tail. The bird measures approximately 22 to 35 inches in length. The head is an irridescent greenish purple, with red wattles around the eye. The body is made up of a variety of brightly colored feathers—mottled beige and reddish with blue tinges. The female lacks the bright colors but also has a long tail and short wings and is mottled brown.

HABITAT AND RANGE: This bird was introduced into this country, and is now widespread from lower Canada across the United States. It is commonly found in fields, meadows, brushy areas, and farms.

The common name ring-necked alludes to the white collar between the neck and breast of the male. The name pheasant is a general term given to about thirty-seven members of this family, which also includes quail, peacocks, and partridges. During breeding season, the brightly colored male pheasants sometimes fight to the death for the attentions of a female, who generally seems oblivious to the commotion.

The word *pheasant* is from a Greek word meaning "bird of the River Phasis." This river, the modern-day Rioni, is found in southeastern Europe and flows from the Caucasus Mountains. At least one species of pheasant is native to this area.

The first ring-necked pheasants were brought to this country from China in the late 1800s. Today in the United States these birds are often bred in captivity and then released as game birds. They are particularly good for hunting because they fly almost vertically when flushed and are not capable of sustaining long flight.

In China the pheasant is considered a thunder, or rain, bird. In order to bring rain, pheasant dances were performed in which the dancers would imitate the movements of the birds and the flapping of its wings. Marcel Garnet, the French orientalist, said, "Thunder is a pheasant."

Golden pheasants were introduced to Europe from China in 1740, and from France, Lafayette sent a pair to George Washington, who kept them at Mount Vernon.

A French manuscript showed a pheasant being trapped by his own reflection in a mirror. European peasantry were not allowed to hunt or hawk, so they had to resort to ingenious methods of catching game. The mirror was a favorite trick.

The green pheasant, believed to be able to predict earthquakes, is the national bird of Japan; the ring-necked pheasant is the state bird of South Dakota.

BAND-TAILED PIGEON

COMMON NAME: Pigeon, Band-tailed

SCIENTIFIC NAME: *Columba fasciata*

DESCRIPTION: A chunky, dovelike bird, the pigeon is about 14 to 16 inches long. It is dark gray all over with a wide, light gray band at the tip of the fantail and a dark band above it. The feet are yellow, the bill yellow with a dark tip. This pigeon looks similar to the domestic rock dove.

HABITAT AND RANGE: This bird is found in mountains, oak and pine woods, canyons, and chaparral from southwest British Columbia throughout the American West, and down into South America.

The name pigeon is from the Latin *pipire*, meaning "to peep," and refers to the soft cooing or hooting of these birds. The species name *fasciata* is from the Latin word for "banded," a reference to the banded tail.

The pigeon is an excellent flier, and has been timed at speeds of over 80 miles an hour. Homing pigeons, even when released hundreds of miles from their roosts, can always find their way home. Experiments have found that these birds actually use the earth's magnetic field to orient themselves.

Homing pigeons have long been used as messengers. In the original Panhellenic games of ancient Greece, homing pigeons were kept ready to fly to notify neighboring cities of the winners. In the old Mongol market, the exchange rate was announced at four-thirty every morning. At this time a flock of pigeons was released to carry news of the current rate to various banks. During World Wars I and II, homing pigeons were used to carry both official and private messages across enemy lines.

These birds feed their young "pigeon milk," a cheese-like substance rich in fat and protein.

The Cherokee Indians tell a legend of former times, when animals talked to one another. When a great famine came and there was no mast (a combination of beechnuts, acorns, and chestnuts), the animals sent the pigeon out to find food. The pigeon returned to say that she had found a country where the people were up to their ankles in mast. Together the animals moved to this rich, low country.

Aesop's fables depict the pigeon as a nimble flyer.

The common pigeon, also known as the rock dove, nests in cliffs when found in the wild. It is more often found, however, in man-made structures, feeding on scraps of grains and bread obtained in the city.

The passenger pigeon, now extinct, was native to North America and was at one time found in tremendous numbers here. These birds flew in large flocks, following ripening fruit in the western parts of the country. John James Audubon wrote that he once watched an enormous flock of pigeons fly past for three days. He estimated that they were flying by at the rate of 300 million per hour.

Passenger pigeons were hunted as food for both men and livestock. Pioneers felt that there must have been an inexhaustible supply of these birds since they observed them in such tremendous flocks. Between the years 1870 and 1899, passenger pigeons were shot and killed in huge numbers, sometimes thousands a day. One source from Michigan reports that in 1874, 25,000 birds were shot every day for nearly a month.

The extinction of the passenger pigeon resulted not only from the direct onslaught of hunting but also from a loss of habitat and breeding ground. As the population began to dwindle, the remaining birds had difficulty reproducing, for the safety of great numbers seemed to be a stimulus to nesting and raising chicks.

The last wild passenger pigeon was thought to have been shot in Wisconsin in 1899. The Wisconsin Society for Ornithology erected a memorial plaque, which reads: "Dedicated to the last Wisconsin passenger pigeon, shot at Babcock September 1899. This species became extinct through the avarice and thoughtlessness of man."

The last captive passenger pigeon died at the Cincinnati Zoo in 1914.

COMMON NAME: Plover, American Golden

SCIENTIFIC NAME: *Pluvialis dominica*

DESCRIPTION: A chunky wading bird, the lesser golden plover is the size of a killdeer, about 10 to 11 inches long. This bird has black underparts, legs, and feet. A white stripe beginning at the crown runs over the eye and beside the neck and breast. The head is dark and the bill black. The back appears to be covered with golden-edged brown shingles.

HABITAT AND RANGE: These birds generally breed on tundra; during migration, on prairies, shorelines, and mud flats.

This species summers in the Arctic regions of North America. In late summer they begin their migration south, which is one of the longest of any bird. The lesser golden plover travels over thousands of miles of open ocean after it leaves the tundra breeding grounds to winter along the coast of South America. The birds take a different migration route in spring, returning to the Arctic by way of the Great Plains. This allows them to take advantage of the abundance of berries and food along the way on their northward trip. The spring migration is done in two phases, which together cover over

AMERICAN GOLDEN PLOVER

20,000 miles. To accomplish the journey is an astounding feat for a bird that weighs only about six ounces.

The name plover is pronounced like *cover,* not *clover.* The common name comes from the golden plumage of the bird.

The natural population of this bird was greatly reduced by hunters. The birds were shot in tremendous numbers and were sold at market as game birds. Luckily, strict enforcement of protection laws has helped the population stabilize, though its full recovery is still in the future.

Plovers are considered "rain birds." Even the name comes from the Latin word *pluv,* which means "rain." It is said that hunters knew there would be golden plovers appearing when there were onshore storms. Some say that these birds were easier to capture in the rain.

Plovers, like killdeers, are well known for their "play acting" to draw predators away from their nest and young. If one approaches, the adult plover will hop away from the nest, dragging a wing or perhaps even both wings, appearing hurt or injured. This way they will expose themselves to danger rather than endanger their young.

COMMON NAME: Prairie Chicken, Greater

SCIENTIFIC NAME: *Tympanuchus cupido*

DESCRIPTION: This bird, which measures 16 to 18 inches in length, is a mottled brown all over and has a heavily barred breast and a white throat. The tip of the short, rounded tail has a wide black band.

HABITAT AND RANGE: The greater prairie chicken is found in native tallgrass prairie and some agricultural lands. Its range includes Canadian and U.S. prairie lands; it is seen in south-central Canada and the north-central United States sporadically as far south as Texas.

Natural populations of the prairie chicken have shrunk drastically as the tallgrass prairies have been reduced. The prairie chicken eats insects found in the grass during summer and seeds and fruits during the winter months.

The courtship ritual of this bird has always fascinated people. The males drum their feet on the ground during the mating dance and, from special inflatable air sacs, emit a boom-ing call that can be heard for many miles. The genus name *Tympanuchus,* a Greek-Latin combination meaning "having a drum," refers to this booming sound.

The species name *cupido,* which was assigned by Linnaeus, derives from Cupid, son of Venus, and is a reference to the little wings on the bird's neck, which were likened to Cupid's wings.

GREATER PRAIRIE CHICKEN

WHITE-TAILED PTARMIGAN

COMMON NAME: Ptarmigan, White-tailed
SCIENTIFIC NAME: *Lagopus leucurus*

DESCRIPTION: A sturdy grouse of high alpine and Arctic tundra, the ptarmigan measures about 12 inches in length. It is pure white in winter, in summer mottled brown and white, with white underparts. During all seasons it has white legs and feet, which are feathered to the toes, and white wings and tail.

HABITAT AND RANGE: This bird practices somewhat of a reverse migration. When other birds are migrating south for the winter, the ptarmigan goes north and to higher altitudes above the treeline, where cold winds blow the ground clear and reveal its winter's food supply. As other birds fly north in spring, the ptarmigan heads for warmer climates, traveling down from the mountain tops to feast on the new growth of the dwarf willow, a staple of the ptarmigan diet. The white-tailed ptarmigan is found in southeast Alaska, western Canada, and scattered locations in the western United States, especially in the Rockies. It is most often seen above the timberline in the alpine tundra, usually in rocky areas with sparse vegetation.

Ptarmigans are so beautifully adapted to their cold environment that they will actually burrow into a snowbank to spend the night. Its mottled spring coloring gives this bird excellent protection, as a motionless bird can hardly be detected beside patches of snow.

The willow ptarmigan feeds almost exclusively on the twigs of willow and alder, which give its flesh a bitter taste. The willow buds actually ferment in the intestine, producing alcohol.

Lagopus is from the Greek word for "hare-footed," a reference to the densely feathered shank and foot of this species. This feathering serves as natural snowshoes for the bird, giving it four times the walking surface of the unfeathered foot.

The name ptarmigan is probably from the Gaelic word *tarmachan,* meaning "moutaineer." The confusing *p* was probably added by a classical scholar in the seventeenth century.

In Japan, the ptarmigan lives on the mountaintops and is considered a "thunder bird." It is sacred to the god of thunder, and pictures of these little birds are sometimes hung in doorways to keep away lightning.

The soft feathers of these birds were at one time used as stuffing for bedding. During the 1930s over 25,000 ptarmigans were exported to England during a single year for this reason.

ATLANTIC PUFFIN

COMMON NAME: Puffin, Atlantic

SCIENTIFIC NAME: *Fratercula arctica*

DESCRIPTION: The puffin is a plump, dark seabird about 12 inches long and with a very large, brightly colored bill. It takes approximately five years for the full adult bill to develop. This bird has dark upper parts and has a white face and white underparts. A noticeable red ring encircles the eye.

HABITAT AND RANGE: This water bird is found in the coastal areas of Maine and casually as far south as New Jersey. It feeds while flying at sea and prefers cliff-backed beaches for nests. For nesting, all puffins excavate a deep hole in wind-blown soil. This burrow keeps the chicks safe from predators while parents are gathering food at sea.

Authorities on puffins estimate that the worldwide natural population of this bird might number approximately 15 million. Sixty per cent of these birds nest around the coast of Iceland; and as many as 300,000 pairs are thought to breed around the coast of Newfoundland, Canada.

Puffins were shot for sport in the 1800s until the natural populations, particularly in the United States, were severely depleted. By 1887 there were no puffins left on Machias Seal Island, formerly the site of their largest colony in Maine. Today, thanks to the reintroduction of these birds and strict enforcement of protection laws, there are more than 1,000 breeding pairs at this site.

Puffins have such distinctive physical characteristics that they have often been the object of affectionate fun from people. This is evident from the number of common names given to this bird, which looks like a waiter dressed in a tuxedo. The name puffin derives either from the "puffed-up" appearance of the adults or from the "powder-puff" appearance of the downy chicks.

Tom Noddy was a name given to the bird in the Farne Islands, in the North Sea. This is similar to Tammie Norie, another local name in the north of England. Coulter Neb is a nickname that refers to the bird's unusual beak. Some other names having to do with its beak are bottlenose, sea parrot, and sea bill. In Yorkshire it was known as the Flamborough head pilot. These birds were also known as Lundi or Lunda, and the Lundy Island in the Bristol Channel was named for the number of puffins that were found here.

Puffins were considered a delicious food in old England and were sold at the rate of three puffins for a penny. The puffin has very little flesh, and it took two or three puffins to make a meal.

The Irish, however, did not eat puffins, as it was believed that the reincarnated spirits of monks lived within these birds.

The genus name, *Fratercula,* is from the Latin for "brother" or "little friar" and could either be a reference to the Irish legend or to the bird's habit when rising from the sea of clasping its feet as though in prayer.

Today the greatest threat to puffins is from ocean oil spills.

CALIFORNIA QUAIL

COMMON NAME: Quail, California
SCIENTIFIC NAME: *Callipepla californica*

DESCRIPTION: This is a small, 10-inch-long, ground-hunting bird that eats insects, seeds and fruits. It lays numerous eggs, sometimes as many as twenty-five in a clutch, in a shallow depression of ground. The male has a distinctive black plume that curves forward from the top of its head. Its back plumage is a soft grayish brown; the throat is black, the breast is gray, and the underparts are "checkered" beige and black. Females are smaller and lack distinctive coloration.

HABITAT AND RANGE: These birds are found on farms, ranches, chaparral, and coastal brush, from the Pacific Coast inland to the Great Salt Lake, and south to Baja California. They were introduced into British Columbia, Canada, from the United States.

The name quail is similar to the word *quack,* and both refer to the noise made by this bird. The origin of these words is from the Dutch *quacken,* meaning "to croak." In old French the word became *quaille.* The genus name *Callipepla* is from the Greek, *kallipeplos,* meaning "beautifully adorned"—from *kalos,* "beautiful," and *peplos,* "ceremonial robe."

Quails were kept by the Romans for food. We also have good evidence that they were well known in Egypt, because their likeness often appears in Egyptian hieroglyphics.

A Christian-era story of Moses says that the Israelites were fed in the desert by enormous flocks of quails that dropped to the ground from the heavens.

According to American Indian legend, the animals elected the crane as the Bird King. This so enraged the quail that a quarrel broke out between the two birds. Finally the crane struck and broke the quail's backbone, so that thereafter the quail always had to fly low. Some say that the crane felt so bad about this that it always carries the quail on its back during migration.

During the Middle Ages in Europe it was sometimes believed that the quail mated with a toad, supposedly because of the (very slight) resemblance between the two. To dream of the quail was thought to mean difficult times were coming.

In China and Malaysia, quailfights were almost as popular as cockfights and are still allowed there today. This practice must have been common in Europe as well, since Shakespeare wrote in *Antony and Cleopatra*: "His cocks do win the battle still of mine, / When it is all to nought; and his quails ever / Beat mine, inhoop'd, at odds. . . ."

Perhaps because of the quail's tenacity and fighting nature, it became symbolic of courage and pugnacity.

In Greece quails were kept as pets and were bred for excellence in song, color, and form. It was the custom for a man to give his lover a pet quail.

The California quail forms large flocks in winter, sometimes as many as 200 birds. They communicate by a loud, crowlike call that helps keep the flock together. The California quail has no true song.

The quail does not build a complicated nest but merely scrapes out a hollow in the ground among brush or in grainfields. Here the male and female raise twelve to eighteen chicks and stay together in a covey (a family group) until fall. This is the state bird of California.

COMMON NAME: Rail, Virginia

SCIENTIFIC NAME: *Rallus limicola*

DESCRIPTION: Rails are medium-sized birds (about 9 inches long), rusty grayish brown in color with moderately long legs adapted for wading. They are characterized by gray cheeks, rusty breast, horizontal barring on underparts, and a long, slender, slightly decurved bill.

HABITAT AND RANGE: This bird frequents fresh, salt, and brackish marshes, hiding among cattails and reeds. It is very secretive and seldom seen. When flushed, it seems to fly only reluctantly, its legs dangling. The rail feeds on aquatic plants, seeds, insects, frogs, and crustaceans. This species winters in coastal areas of the eastern United States north to Virginia and occasionally beyond.

The name rail probably came from the bird's distinctive cry, perhaps from the Latin word *raelare,* meaning "to scrape." The species name, *limicola,* is from the Latin for "mud-dweller," a reference to the preferred habitat of this bird.

In Scotland, local superstition held that if a rail circled over a field and cried, it meant someone nearby would soon die.

In the Palau Islands in the Pacific Ocean, the rail was considered an evil deity and was thought to bring disease and death.

"Thin as a rail" is an expression that may have originated with reference to this bird. It is long and slender, well camouflaged amid the reeds of the marsh.

Many members of the rail family have completely lost the ability to fly. In Hawaii, the Laysan Island rail, unable to fly and protect itself, was wiped out by rats that arrived there on ships during World War II.

VIRGINIA RAIL

COMMON RAVEN

COMMON NAME: Raven, Common

SCIENTIFIC NAME: *Corvus corax*

DESCRIPTION: The raven is a big (17 to 21 inches long), chunky, all-black bird; it is larger than the American crow. In flight the tail shows a wedge shape. In bright sunshine the raven's glossy coat shows a hint of purple. The heavy bill and feet are black and the voice is more guttural and lower than the crow's caw.

HABITAT AND RANGE: The raven is commonly found in Alaska, where it endures the Arctic winter, across Canada, and throughout the western United States, extending also into Mexico. A small number can also be found in the Appalachian Mountains. These large birds are widespread in mountain forests, tundra, farms, and suburban areas.

Glossy black, large, and imposing, the raven has always been an object of superstition and lore. The raven has been considered a trickster in many cultures throughout the world. Trickster myths are part of the cultures of ancient Greeks, Chinese, Japanese, and Semites. In these myths the trickster has universal appeal. He is at the same time creator and destroyer, giver and negator, he tricks and is tricked himself. As a central character of these myths, he is at the mercy of his appetites and his passions. The raven is perpetually led by his voracious appetite into many violent and amorous adventures.

The raven cycle is a collection of trickster-transformer tales popular among the Native Americans of the Pacific Northwest. The cycle begins with a boy's birth and his early adventures, and continues with his seduction of the daughter of the Sky Chief. To escape the flood that results from his escapades, he must fly to the heavens. Raven, his child, falls to earth and is then adopted by a chief. As an adult, Raven transforms the earth from a dark, dry place to a land with rivers and mountains, people and animals.

The raven has a prominent place in many Native American creation stories. In Tlingit Indian legend, the grandfather of the raven and the mythological chief of the raven clan is a figure they call Raven-at-the-Head-of-Nass ("Nass" being the Nass River). It was he who brought mankind into being, making people out of a rock and a leaf. He showed the leaf to the new people and said, "See this leaf? You are to be like it. When it falls from the branch and rots, there is nothing left of it." Thus he also brought death into the world.

The raven was also thought to have released the sun and moon to their places in the sky and so made daylight. One of the most well-known of all raven myths tells how the sun was hidden away in the lodge of the Sky Chief, so that the world was in perpetual darkness. Raven, determined to get the sun back, changed himself into a spruce needle and floated down the river. The daughter of the Sky Chief swallowed the needle and later gave birth to a baby who was actually the raven himself. As the child grew, he begged and begged his mother to allow him to play with the sun. When she finally agreed, the raven changed back to a bird and, taking the sun, returned to the sky and brought light to the world.

Another legend suggests that the sun, creator of all things, thought the raven the smartest of all animals. The Blackfoot Indians considered the raven a very wise bird and watched him carefully because he was thought to be able to forecast the future. A raven circling high over camp meant that a messenger from far away would soon come bearing news.

On a buffalo hunt, Indians would follow two ravens playing together on a ridge, for that is the direction the buffalo would take. On a war expedition, two ravens with their heads together on the path ahead meant that the enemy was approaching.

Among the Cherokee tribes, the Raven-

mocker was a dreaded figure. The Raven-mocker robbed weak and ill people of their life. According to superstition, when someone was ill and dying, the Raven-mocker would swoop into the village, wings outstretched, and, unless there was a medicine man there to scare him away, would snatch the life of the sick person.

In Europe, too, the raven was considered a mystical and magical bird. Alexander the Great was said to have been guided across the desert by two ravens sent from heaven. In Scotland if a raven circled a house it was understood that someone inside was soon to die.

The raven was loathed throughout Europe as a symbol of impending death and war, probably because it fed on battlefield corpses. In Britain, however, legend maintains that England will not fall as long as ravens live in the Tower of London.

COMMON NAME: Redstart, American
SCIENTIFIC NAME: *Setophaga ruticilla*

DESCRIPTION: A small, glossy black warbler measuring about 5 inches in length, the American redstart is misnamed, for the patches on the wings and tail are more a bright orange than true red. The bird frequently fans its tail and spreads its wings to reveal white underparts. Showing off its bright orange-patched wings, it almost looks like a giant butterfly. The female is olive-gray with yellow patches and white below.

HABITAT AND RANGE: The American redstart lives in southern Canada and in scattered areas of the northwestern United States in addition to the East and the South. It is rarely found in Florida. It frequents stream- and riverbanks and high woodland areas (usually elevations of 5,000 feet or more). It winters in Mexico and South America.

AMERICAN REDSTART

The common name refers to the patches on the outer sides of the tail. It may be a variation of the Old German name *Rothstert,* meaning "red tail." The genus name *Setophaga* is Greek for "insect eater."

The natural population of redstarts is decreasing rapidly as a result of habitat destruction in the rainforests, where they winter, as well as in their breeding grounds in North America.

In Latin America this small bird is known as *candelita,* "little candle" or "little torch." These birds always seem to be in motion, and dance like tiny lights. It takes a full year for the brilliant plumage of the males to develop.

Redstarts feed on flying insects and are capable of catching their prey in flight.

COMMON NAME: Roadrunner, Greater

SCIENTIFIC NAME: *Geococcyx californianus*

DESCRIPTION: Because of its cartoon fame, the roadrunner is easily identified even by people with little knowledge of birds. This bird measures about 22 inches in length and is slender and streaked with brown and white. The long brown tail is edged with white and there is white on the wings. The legs are conspicuously long. Both the male and the female look alike. This bird lives up to its name, as it seems to be always running from place to place.

HABITAT AND RANGE: The roadrunner, which does not migrate, lives in the arid Southwest and south into Mexico. It prefers areas with some cover, such as mesquite, and sometimes wanders into mountainous areas. Roadrunners hunt rodents, insects, snakes, and lizards.

Thanks to the world of animation, the roadrunner is a well-known creature. He is most often shown in cartoons outsmarting his archrival, Wile E. Coyote, calling "Beep-beep" just before he speeds by in a cloud of dust.

The roadrunner is capable of flying but seems to prefer to run, perhaps because it can do so at a speed of 15 miles per hour. He is often associated with the cuckoo, presumably on account of his terrestrial proclivities. The genus name *Geococcyx* is Greek for "ground cuckoo." The Mexicans call this bird *paisano,* or "countryman."

Southwest Indian legends tell of roadrunners that built walls of cactus around sleeping rattlesnakes. When the snakes awoke, they would thrash around and stab themselves to death on the sharp spines of the cactus. Roadrunners do eat snakes, even rattlesnakes, but none have been known to catch them in this legendary manner.

Other common names for this bird include chapparal cock, ground cuckoo, and snake killer. The roadrunner is the state bird of New Mexico.

GREATER ROADRUNNER

AMERICAN ROBIN

COMMON NAME: Robin, American

SCIENTIFIC NAME: *Turdus migratorius*

DESCRIPTION: The well-known robin is 9 to 11 inches long and has a dark head, gray-brown back and wings, and a black tail. Its breast is a brick-red color and black streaks appear on its throat. The female is similar but has softer colors. The young have speckled breasts.

HABITAT AND RANGE: Robins are found in residential areas, towns, and gardens. In the northern hemisphere they are found from Alaska and Canada south throughout the United States and Mexico. They prefer to nest near human habitation in rain gutters, mail boxes, and shade trees.

The robin's red breast once marked him as sacred. In many cultures it was believed that if you harmed it or its nest, you would be struck by lightning, or your cow would get sick and give bloody milk.

British superstition suggested that to break a robin's leg meant that soon you would break an arm or leg. To break open a robin's egg would cause something belonging to the culprit to be broken. In Wales if you harmed a robin, it was thought that you would be punished by witches and warlocks. In Devon a local saying warned: "Kill a robin or a wren—never prosper, boy or man."

Some superstitions considered the robin a bringer of death or bad luck. In Suffolk, a robin entering a house meant death to the inhabitants, and a robin that pecked at a window was a forerunner to disaster.

The robin was also thought to foretell the weather. If it sang high in the trees, fair weather was supposed to follow, but if a robin stayed close to a house all autumn, a harsh winter was thought to lie ahead.

In some cultures it was believed that the robin brought fire, because of its fiery red breast.

The early nineteenth-century American poet John Greenleaf Whittier wrote these lines about robins, which are based on a Welsh tale about how the robin helps people:

> *"Nay" said Grandmother, "have you not heard*
> *My poor bad boy, of the fiery pit,*
> *And how drop by drop this merciful bird*
> *Carries the water that quenches it?*
> *He brings cool dew in his little bill*
> *And lets it fall on the souls of men*
> *You can see the marks on his red breast still*
> *Of the fires that scorch as he drops it in."*

Legend tells us that the robin received its red breast when it plucked a thorn from Christ's crown on his way to Calvary and the flowing blood turned his breast feathers red.

In more modern folklore, Tin Pan Alley in New York City produced a song in praise of "the red, red robin" that came "bob-bob-bobbin' along."

The name Robin was a favorite affectionate nickname for Robert and was first given to the European "Robin Redbreast." The American robin is in a different genus but was given the same nickname by the early American pioneers.

Shakespeare invoked ancient folklore when he wrote in *Cymbeline* that the robin would cover an unburied body with moss.

In northern states, spring is said to arrive with the robins. Each year robins head north from their southern wintering grounds and return to the location where they were fledged.

The American robin is the official state bird of Connecticut, Michigan, and Wisconsin.

COMMON NAME: Sandpiper, Curlew

SCIENTIFIC NAME: *Calidris ferruginea*

OTHER SPECIES: Semipalmated sandpiper (*Calidris pusilla*) and solitary sandpiper (*Tringa solitaria*)

DESCRIPTION: In summer this 8-inch bird has a red breast and a brownish rust back, a long, slender decurved bill, and brownish stripes on its head. The semipalmated sandpiper is slightly smaller, measuring 6 inches, with a distinctive white stripe that shows on the wings in flight. The solitary sandpiper is a darker bird with bold bars on the tail, also best seen when the bird is in flight. After it lands this bird bobs its tail up and down. During winter it is gray and white.

HABITAT AND RANGE: Running above the breaking waves to search for tiny crustaceans and marine life, the curlew sandpiper is rare in America but can be found on sandy beaches in Alaska, on islands of the Bering Sea, in southwestern Canada, and in the northwestern United States. The semipalmated sandpiper breeds in Alaska and migrates across the eastern United States to winter on the Gulf Coast. It is considered an abundant shorebird of both fresh and salt waters. The solitary sandpiper is commonly found in swamps, lakes, and streams.

There is great variation among sandpipers. They differ in size from a few inches to 2 feet and can have rather short, stocky legs, or long slender ones. Most are sand- or earth-colored. Sandpipers can be found throughout the world, including Arctic regions.

Along with many other shorebirds, sandpipers were hunted and shot in distressingly great numbers. Thanks to protective laws,

CURLEW SANDPIPER

however, most natural populations have begun to recover.

The name *Calidris* was used by Aristotle in reference to a "speckled gray shorebird." *Ferruginea* is Latin for "rusty red," referring to the color in breeding season. The genus name *Tringa* is from the Greek for "water bird with a white rump," and *solitaria* is Latin for "solitary," which describes the reclusive nature of this bird.

COMMON NAME: Sapsucker, Yellow-bellied

SCIENTIFIC NAME: *Sphyrapicus varius*

DESCRIPTION: As its name suggests, this bird has a blush of yellow on its breast. Its back is black with a long white patch; its wings also have a white patch. It has a red throat and crown and a strong chisel-like bill. The female is similar but with more muted colors and a white throat.

HABITAT AND RANGE: The yellow-bellied sapsucker breeds across Canada and throughout the United States with the exception of the west-central states. It travels widely during migration. These birds prefer deciduous woods.

Although unlike other woodpeckers, this species does not drum when excavating, it does have a distinct rhythm as it drills parallel rows of small holes in live trees, to which it returns later to feed on the sap and insects. This sap makes up about 20 percent of its diet, the remainder coming from small insects and berries. (When hummingbirds migrate before nectar is available from flowering plants, they, too, will feed from the sapsucker's drillings.)

The name sapsucker is given to the three members of the woodpecker family that nest and breed in North America. The tongues of sapsuckers are shorter than other woodpeckers, and are covered with fine hairs that allow them to retrieve the sap more easily.

The family name Picidae is the Latin word for "woodpecker." It derives from Picus, the son of Saturn who was transformed into a woodpecker by Circe when he rejected her love.

YELLOW-BELLIED SAPSUCKER

NORTHERN SHRIKE

COMMON NAME: Shrike, Northern
SCIENTIFIC NAME: *Lanius excubitor*

DESCRIPTION: Measuring 9 inches long, the northern shrike has pale gray back and head, a black mask, black wings, and a black tail edged in white. When in flight, the bird shows a distinctive white patch on its underwing. Its black bill is hooked at the tip. The sexes are similarly colored.

HABITAT AND RANGE: This bird breeds in Alaska and northern Canada and winters in Alaska and northwestern Canada and across southern Canada and the northern United States. It feeds on rodents, snakes, small birds, and insects and prefers open country with occasional trees or posts, which it uses as lookout stations.

The shrike is called the "butcher bird" because of its habit of impaling its prey on a large thorn or point of barbed wire to hold it until it gets hungry again. The family name, Laniidae, is from the Latin for "butcher," a reference to this practice.

Excubitor is Latin for "watchman," or "sentinel." Linnaeus justified this name by explaining that the shrike "looks out for the approach of hawks and warns little birds." But as the shrike actually feeds on small birds, this explanation seems a little absurd.

Thoreau, kindly overlooking the shrike's butcherlike characteristics, described this bird's song as "with heedless and unfrozen melody bringing back summer again."

The shrike was sometimes called the messenger bird and also the French mockingbird. The Zuni considered it a brilliant bird but an evil one. According to a tale told in Madagascar, the shrike was at one time elected "king of all the birds."

A European legend about a hawk and a shrike is a variation of the tortoise and the hare story. The hawk and shrike have a race, and the shrike finally wins due to his perseverance.

COMMON SNIPE

COMMON NAME: Snipe, Common
SCIENTIFIC NAME: *Gallinago gallinago*

DESCRIPTION: Slightly larger than a robin, the snipe is about 11 inches long and has a brownish back with beige vertical stripes. Long buff-brown stripes are found on the breast, which has white underparts. The long bill is blunt at the end. The snipe flies in a zigzag fashion.

HABITAT AND RANGE: The snipe breeds in bogs, marshes, or any moist areas throughout northern North America. This bird is frequently seen on top of fence posts.

The name snipe means "snipper," or "snapper," and refers to the beak, which is used to snap up food. It may also describe the snapping sound made by the beak.

This species was formerly called Wilson's snipe, after the eighteenth-century ornithologist Alexander Wilson. The genus and species names come from the Latin *gallina,* meaning "hen."

The male courtship dance is performed during the breeding season at dusk or on moonlit nights and involves the bird's flying almost straight up into the air almost 300 feet and then zigzagging down to earth, fascinating not only the female snipes but any humans fortunate enough to observe it. The air flowing over the feathers produces an eerie whistle that is commonly called winnowing, or bleating.

Henry David Thoreau, who often witnessed the male in its bleating courtship rite, described it as "fanning the air like a spirit over some far meadow's bay."

The snipe is called *so-otak-skan,* or "shad-

ow in the water," by the Blackfoot Indians. They gave it this name because the snipe is known to stand in shallow water, admiring its own reflection.

In a favorite story told by the Cochita Indians, the toad and the snipe were playing hide-and-seek. The snipe hid in the river sand, but could not bury all of her long bill, which stuck out of the sand. The toad searched and searched for her until he ran into her bill. He grabbed it and called out, "I've found an awl for Grandfather to fix his shoes," and pulled and pulled until the snipe popped out of the sand.

According to the Hopi Indians, the snipe is one of the cloud's pets and an important water symbol. Their name for it is *patsro,* or "water bird." The snipe was thought to have the power to bring together the horned water serpent, who controls the underground waterways, the Germinator, who sends crops from the underground, and the Sky God, who sends down lightning and rain.

Hunters have always found snipes difficult

to shoot because of their erratic flight pattern. Even so, one nineteenth-century hunter boasted that he had killed 340 snipes in a single day and that he almost always got 150 a day through the fall, winter, and spring. Their numbers are not so great as they once were but are high enough that it is legal to hunt them in many areas.

COMMON NAME: Sparrow, Song
SCIENTIFIC NAME: *Melospiza melodia*

DESCRIPTION: Song sparrows vary widely in color and size. The Aleutian variety of the song sparrow is large and dark. In the desert the song sparrow is pale in color and quite small. A typical western song sparrow is a mottled brown on the back and head; the beak is whitish with small streaks, and there is one large, dark brown spot in the center of the breast.

HABITAT AND RANGE: Song sparrows are abundant throughout most of Canada and the United States. These seed-eating birds frequent open areas, cultivated gardens, and roadsides.

Many ancient peoples believed that sparrows sprang from horsehair and mud. According to superstition, the sparrow guards fire for the devil and chases the swallow who steals the fire and takes it to man.

The genus name *Melospiza* is from the Greek words *melos,* meaning "song," and *spiza,* meaning "finch." The male sparrow is said to have as many as twenty different melodies. The Blackfoot Indians called the white-throated sparrows "summer-bringers" and believed that the message of their song was: "The leaves are budding and summer is coming."

Many people believed that if the sparrow chirps with exceptional enthusiasm, it is a sign that it will rain soon. The Chinese considered the sparrow a supernatural messenger and a foreteller of good luck. In Japan a sparrow pictured under a maple tree was a symbol of gentleness, gratitude, and joy.

The sparrow was a Hindu symbol of fruitfulness and fertility; and in Rome, the sparrow was sacred to Venus.

SONG SPARROW

In Robert Browning's poem for children, "The Pied Piper," sparrows get top billing:

The sparrows were brighter than peacocks here
And the dogs outran the fallow deer
And honey bees had lost their stings,
And horses were born with eagle's wings.

Geoffrey Chaucer, author of *The Canterbury Tales,* considered the sparrow lecherous.

Cherokee Indians call the bird *tsiskwaya,* meaning "main, or principal bird," because it was found in so many different places.

COMMON NAME: Spoonbill, Roseate
SCIENTIFIC NAME: *Ajaia ajaja*

DESCRIPTION: Measuring 30 to 32 inches, the spoonbill has long, bright pink legs. Its unusual bill is long and spoon-shaped at the tip. The bill moves from side to side in a swinging motion in shallow salt water as the spoonbill searches for food. The head is bare, and light greenish in color. The body is pink, the back and neck white.

HABITAT AND RANGE: Along the coasts of the Gulf of Mexico and much of Florida, the roseate spoonbill nests in colonies, often mixed in with other large wading birds. This large bird can be seen wading in shallow coastal waters.

Both the genus and species names are variations of the Brazilian name for this bird, which, in turn, is based on a Greek word for "sacred bird." The names were awarded to this family of birds because it includes the ibis, which was considered sacred. "Roseate" refers to the bright pink plumage found on this species. The name spoonbill, of course, refers to the unusual shape of the bill.

Until early in this century, the pink feathers of this bird were used extensively for adorning ladies' hats, a practice that threatened the native populations of the spoonbill. Legal protection is responsible for its comeback.

The inside of the bill is lined with sensitive tissue that feels food as the birds swish their beaks through the water.

ROSEATE SPOONBILL

EUROPEAN STARLING

COMMON NAME: Starling, European
SCIENTIFIC NAME: *Sturnus vulgaris*

DESCRIPTION: An 8-inch, iridescent black bird, the European starling has a large, sharp, pointed bill. Its winter plumage is speckled; the sexes are similarly colored.

HABITAT AND RANGE: Found across Canada and the United States, the starling was introduced to this country in 1890 from Great Britain.

There are more European starlings in the world than any other bird. From its native Europe it has been introduced to all four corners of the globe, from Australia to North America, from Asia to the Pacific Islands.

The starling first came to this country in 1890, the result of a group of Shakespeare enthusiasts who sought to bring to America every bird ever mentioned by the bard. Unfortunately, the starling was among them. Starlings adapted quickly and soon spread across the country.

Harry Power of Rutgers University said, "Starlings are much more like us than bluebirds are. In fact, when we look at them, to some extent we're looking at a morality play of ourselves."

And it is not always a play that makes us feel good about ourselves. Male birds get into knock-down-drag-out fights over females and nesting sites. Egg parasitism and nest stealing are also prevalent. They even kill their own kind—for example, in winter they will kill for the chance to roost in a nest box. Studies show that their murder rate may be as high as 10 percent.

The starling has many undesirable habits. It keeps an untidy nest, deposits droppings on sidewalks and patios, and is noisy. Starlings are also disliked for their habit of driving away bluebirds from their nesting boxes and competing for existing cavities in trees or in saguaro cactus.

In 1960 an airliner crashed, killing sixty-two people, as a result of running through a flock of starlings, which effectively destroyed the engine.

Starlings, like mockingbirds, are able to mimic the songs and calls of many different birds. The name starling was, perhaps, given to this bird because some people believed that the bird in flight was star-shaped.

WOOD STORK

COMMON NAME: Stork, Wood

SCIENTIFIC NAME: *Mycteria americana*

DESCRIPTION: The wood stork is a very large, white-bodied wading bird measuring nearly 40 inches in length. It has a large band of black on the trailing edge of the wing and a short black tail. Its naked head is grayish black and the thick bill is curved on the end. When it flies, the wood stork extends its neck, but while feeding, it keeps its neck down as it wades, searching for food.

HABITAT AND RANGE: This bird breeds from Florida and the Gulf Coast south to Argentina, occasionally wandering to other spots in South America. They frequent marshes, ponds, and coastal areas, feeding on fish, reptiles, and amphibians. They make their nests in trees.

The wood stork, formerly known as the wood ibis, is the only stork native to North America. Unfortunately, the population of this bird is decreasing due to loss of habitat, earning it a place on the federal endangered species list. The wood stork nests high in the uppermost branches of bald cypress trees in swamps and marshes.

The word *wood* was included in the name because it refers to the species' preference for perching and resting in trees. Also, when the bird's mandibles come together, it sounds like two pieces of wood striking each other.

The name stork has been in existence for thousands of years. A Scandinavian legend tells us that when Christ was on the cross, the stork flew around crying *"styrket, styrket"*— "Strengthen ye." The origin of the name is probably from the word *stark,* meaning strong, a description of the rigid posture of storks.

The genus name *Mycteria* is from the Greek for "snout," a reference to the bird's long bill.

Thoth, the Egyptian god of wisdom and learning, is pictured as a man with the head of an ibis or wood stork. The sacred ibis, *Threskiornis aethiopica,* was sacred to the ancient Egyptians.

In Germany the stork is a symbol of filial devotion. According to legend, the Eurasian white stork carries babies from heaven and delivers them to their mothers' laps.

On Tenos, an island in the Aegean Sea, tradition has it that Poseidon, Greek god of the sea, sent the stork to clear the island of snakes.

WILSON'S STORM PETREL

COMMON NAME: Storm Petrel, Wilson's

SCIENTIFIC NAME: *Oceanites oceanicus*

DESCRIPTION: A 7-inch-long, brownish black water bird, the storm petrel seems to dance over the waves. It has a rounded white rump patch that extends under the tail. The tail is not forked but is square on the end. It has webbed feet and a sturdy hooked beak. Its tubular nostrils are used for removing salt from seawater. Glands separate the salt, which then leaves the body through tubes.

HABITAT AND RANGE: Except during the breeding season, Wilson's storm petrel spends all of its time at sea. These birds eat plankton, fish, and shrimp and often follow ships for their refuse. They breed in the Antarctic region but are common off the Atlantic Coast from May to September, and are rarely seen along the California coast.

Considered one of the most abundant birds in the world, this species nests by the millions in the Southern Hemisphere, traveling to the Northern Hemisphere for our summer months.

The genus name *Oceanites* is Greek for "son of the sea," or more specifically, "son of the sea god, Oceanus." Hydrobatidae, the family name, is from the Greek words for "water walking."

Wilson's storm petrels are said to look as if they were hovering on top of the water, or maybe even walking on it. The bird was named for Saint Peter because of the belief that it truly could walk on water.

The common name, storm petrel, comes from the fact that during high winds and heavy seas these birds usually fly in the wake of the waves or of any other large object at sea. During storms they may appear suddenly beside a ship or boat.

The nickname "Mother Carey's Chickens" may have come from the invocation *mata cara* (dear mother), often spoken by sailors seeking help in a storm. Another tradition explains that Mother Carey, a witch of the sea, was always followed by these small black birds.

The "Wilson" of this name is the Scottish-born American ornithologist, Alexander Wilson (1766–1813).

The storm petrel does not build a nest but lays a single large white egg in a rocky crevice. Both the male and the female share the incubation duties.

BARN SWALLOW

COMMON NAME: Swallow, Barn
SCIENTIFIC NAME: *Hirundo rustica*

DESCRIPTION: Small, with a deeply forked tail, the barn swallow reaches a length of only 5³/₄ to 7³/₄ inches. The throat and forehead are a rusty brown, the underparts all creamy white, and the upperparts a dark steel-blue.

HABITAT AND RANGE: Barn swallows breed in almost every state, with the exception of Florida and Hawaii. They are found near lakeshores and marshy areas, in agricultural lands, and in suburban areas.

Barn swallows originally built their nests in rocky crevices or ledges or tree trunks near water, but now situate them almost exclusively in buildings, thus the common name. They lay four to six brown-spotted white eggs in a nest, which is usually a solid cup of mud with a lining of grass, hay, or some other plant material.

Barn swallows migrate tremendous distances, some going as far as from the northern United States to Argentina. They generally restrict their flying to daytime and sometimes cover as many as 600 miles daily.

The swallow is much beloved in England, where it is a sign that summer is on the way. In ancient Greece, where the bird was considered sacred to the household gods, a swallow festival was held every spring. Greek women would catch a swallow, anoint it with oil, and then set it free to remove any ill luck. The nests of these birds were supposed to bring luck. So dear were swallows to the people of Italy that a decree of 1496 protected these birds from harm.

Swallows were not always considered a symbol of good luck, however. In Germany peasants believed that many swallows perching on a house foretold poverty there. If a swallow flew beneath a man's arm or under a cow, it was believed that the man would lose a limb and that the cow would sicken and die. In Ireland it is said that the swallow is the devil's bird, and in Scotland it was thought that the swallow carried a drop of blood from the devil.

According to legends from many Eastern countries, the swallow was thought to have brought fire to man. In one story, the forked tail and red markings of some species of swallow were the result of the devil throwing a firebrand at the swallow as it flew off with a bit of fire. The Jews of Turkey believed that the swallow brought water to put out the fire in the Temple in Jerusalem and that the bird has shown blackened feathers ever since.

In China swallows are considered lucky. Chinese peasants, when they prayed for rain, sometimes tried to attract the attention of the gods by catching swallows by the river. When the swallows arrived in spring, an offering was made to the household gods so that the women of the house would be blessed with fertility, and if a swallow entered the home, it was taken as an omen of prosperity. In China, twittering women are often likened to swallows.

In many Eastern cultures, the swallow was used medicinally. A divine concoction was made with aromatic herbs and swallows. This mixture was thought to have supernatural healing powers.

In the seventeenth century, a treatment for epilepsy was made with 100 swallows, an ounce of castor oil, and white wine. An ancient folk cure for the bite of a mad dog included dung from a badger, a cuckoo, and a swallow.

The following legend is often told about swallows and ravens:

The little swallow lost her husband and stood mourning him when the raven came by and asked what was wrong. She answered that she was weeping for her husband, who was now dead. The raven said to her, "Take me instead. I am strong." But the swallow merely shook her head no. The raven, sad and lonely, saw a flock of geese flying south and decided to fly off with them. He could not keep up, however, and finally fell into the ocean from exhaustion. His body disintegrated and was changed into little black mollusks that today we call sea ravens.

Much symbolism is associated with the swallow. To dream of this bird meant family happiness. Conversely, if one dreamed of a dead swallow it meant lost affection. In heraldry, the swallow represented one who is prompt and ready, or perhaps the bringer of good news. Swallows were sometimes thought of as a symbol of travel.

Its frail nest was a symbol of danger and insecurity. As a Christian symbol, the young swallow was used to indicate one crying out for spirituality.

COMMON NAME: Swan, Mute
SCIENTIFIC NAME: *Cygnus olor*

DESCRIPTION: This swan is all white and has a bright orange beak that tips down and has a black knob at the base. It holds its neck in a distinctive S curve and carries the wings arched back. The tundra swan, formerly called the whistling swan, measures about 53 inches in length. It migrates in a long line or in a V formation. Unlike the mute swan, the tundra swan holds its neck straight and its wings flat against the body. It has a black bill and black webbed feet.

HABITAT AND RANGE: The mute swan, which was introduced to the United States from Europe, is now found on park lakes and ponds throughout the country.

MUTE SWAN

Swans have been revered for many centuries. Figures of these birds carved into stone have been found dating back to 400 B.C. Swans were considered supernatural and capable of magical powers and many myths and legends developed around them.

According to one Greek myth, the soul of Apollo, god of prophecy, light, youth, music, and poetry, passed into a swan. An ancient superstition holds that when the soul of a dead person enters a bird it is one way of assuring the immortality of the soul and the eventual return to life among men.

During the Golden Age of Greece, it was commonly believed that a swan would sing only just before his death, thus the origin of the expression "swan song." In the *Phaedo,* Plato gives Socrates' last words before he drank the hemlock: "You know that when swans feel the approach of death, they sing—and they sing sweeter and louder on the last days of their lives because they are going back to that god whom they serve."

Shakespeare, also, referred to this in *Othello* when he wrote: "I will play the swan and die in music. / A swan-like end, fading in music."

In Greek mythology Leda, a mortal, was loved by Zeus, who approached her in the form of a swan. Leda gave birth to Castor and Pollux, who spent alternate days among the gods and on the earth.

The swan also played a prominent part in the days of King Arthur. The Swan Knight was a mythical figure who supposedly departed Arthur's court for Nimwegan, Holland, arriving there in a boat pulled by a swan.

From the twelfth to the sixteenth century, swans were held sacred in England. On Whitsunday, 1306, Edward I held the Feast of the Swan, which was considered the most beautiful and elaborate celebration since the legendary coronation of King Arthur.

A German fairy tale tells of a swan-maiden, a creature half human, half supernatural, who is released from her swan body by the talisman of her lover—but changed back to a swan when her lover is unfaithful to her.

Stories and legends of swans are common in Aryan mythology. Both the Grimm brothers and Hans Christian Andersen retold stories about swans.

Swans were considered sacred to Freyr, the Swedish God of the Fruitful Land, Lord of Rain and Sunshine. Swans flying against the blue sky reminded Freyr of fleecy white clouds, which were his home.

In Wales swans were associated with weather. Their eggs were thought to be hatched by thunder and lightning. The name swan is from the Sanskrit word for "sound."

Today the swan is still considered graceful and beautiful but has lost some of its charm because it is so destructive to the environment. Mute swans are overstaying their welcome and becoming quite a problem in some areas. This species was introduced to North America from Europe in the early 1900s. In some states its population is increasing by 30 to 40 percent annually. Rhode Island's Division of Fish and Wildlife spends one month each year seeking out and "shaking" mute swan eggs, thus destroying their viability. This is the only effective means of controlling the population. The number of feral mute swans in the Atlantic Flyway has swollen to more than 6,000, a growth rate in some states of about 40 percent. The birds can live fifty years, and a pair often take over an entire pond.

Swans were historically symbols of wealth and royalty in Europe. In Great Britain ownership of mute swans was, and is, controlled by the Crown, which even has a Royal Swanherd to organize the annual swan roundup, called swan-upping. By the turn of the century, budding American "aristocrats" were importing swan pairs from Britain as symbols of prestige.

Yet as beautiful as they are, a single pair of mute swans can have a significant detrimental impact on aquatic vegetation in an area.

CHIMNEY SWIFT

COMMON NAME: Swift, Chimney

SCIENTIFIC NAME: *Chaetura pelagica*

DESCRIPTION: Measuring about 5 inches in length, the chimney swift has a short, squared tail and a flattened crown. It flies quickly, in spurts. The wings are long and pointed and are swept back.

HABITAT AND RANGE: Found in southeastern Canada and throughout the United States east of the Rockies, chimney swifts live up to their name by frequently nesting in chimneys. Even during migration, flocks will funnel into chimneys at dusk.

Swift is an apt name for this bird, for it can attain amazing speeds. Some members of this species have been clocked at over 100 miles per hour. The bird's anatomy is geared toward flight almost completely; its small feet are largely ineffective for land travel. The family name alludes to this fact: *Apodidae* is from the Latin for "footless." The genus name *Chaetura* is Greek for "spine-tailed," a reference to the spines that project from the ends of the tail feathers.

These birds depend on flying insects for food. During stormy weather when insects do not fly, the chimney swift goes into temporary dormancy, its bodily functions nearly shutting down, and thus requiring little food.

The chimney swift uses its sticky saliva to glue nesting material together and to attach it to the side of a chimney or silo.

A cousin of the chimney swift, the African palm swift, uses its saliva to glue a small bunch of feathers to the end of a palm leaf still attached to the living tree. When the eggs are laid, these are glued to the feathers and the swift spends the next two weeks incubating them.

The western counterpart to the chimney swift is Vaux's swift, which inhabits towns, cities, and mountainous areas. The black swift is larger than the chimney swift and flies at higher altitudes, earning the nickname "cloud swift."

The Reader's Digest *Book of North American Birds* suggests that a long-lived chimney swift may cover more than a million miles before it dies.

SCARLET TANAGER

COMMON NAME: Tanager, Scarlet
SCIENTIFIC NAME: *Piranga olivacea*
OTHER SPECIES: Summer tanager (*Piranga rubra*)

DESCRIPTION: The male of this species is a brilliant red bird with black wings and a black tail. The female is dull, greenish yellow above, pale yellow below. When the birds molt in the fall, the male is a splotchy red color. Both male and female are approximately 7 1/2 inches in length.

HABITAT AND RANGE: The scarlet tanager prefers coniferous or mixed woodlands and depends on insects and fruits for food. These birds are found in the southern portion of eastern Canada and in the United States east of the Mississippi and north of the lower southern states. They winter in South America. Summer tanagers frequent deciduous woods (particularly forests of oak in the East, cottonwoods in the West, and pine groves in the South). They live in the southern half of the southwestern states, as well as in the southeast and Texas.

The name tanager is from the Tupi Indian word for this bird. *Olivacea* is Latin for "olive-colored," a reference to the color of the back of the female. The male's molt is to olive as well.

"Scarlet" refers to the plumage of the males during the breeding season. It appears all red except for the wings and tail. *Rubra* is Latin for "ruby-red," a reference to the color of the wings.

A favorite nickname for the summer tanager is "red beebird," as it is able to overtake flying bees and other insects. Scarlet tanagers are able to eat a tremendous number of insect pests. One bird was observed to eat 600 tent caterpillars in fifteen minutes.

GREEN-WINGED TEAL

COMMON NAME: Teal, Green-winged

SCIENTIFIC NAME: *Anas crecca*

OTHER SPECIES: Cinnamon teal (*Anas cyanoptera*)

DESCRIPTION: The green-winged teal is easily identified by a vertical white bar near the shoulder. The bird measures 14 inches in length and has a grayish body with a green patch on the trailing edge of the wing. The head, throat, and nape are a rusty cinnamon color with a patch of iridescent green that starts at the eye and forms a wide stripe down the side of the head. The female is white below, mottled brown above.

HABITAT AND RANGE: This bird is a surface feeder that inhabits wetlands throughout Alaska, Canada, and the United States with the exception of the Appalachian Mountain region. It feeds in saltwater marshes and in freshwater rivers and inlets.

The genus name *Anas* is from the Latin for "duck," possibly from the verb *natare,* "to swim." The common name teal means "generation" and was given to this bird in connection with its breeding practices. "Green-winged" indicates the green speculum.

The cinnamon teal displays a behavior called "delayed incubation." Instead of starting to incubate the eggs as soon as they are laid, the hen will begin her incubation period only after all the eggs have been laid. This causes the eggs to hatch within a few hours of each other, allowing the chicks to leave the nest together.

Because the green-winged teal is one of the fastest fliers of all ducks, it is a popular game bird.

COMMON TERN

COMMON NAME: Tern, Common
SCIENTIFIC NAME: *Sterna hirundo*

DESCRIPTION: The tern, about 14 inches long, has a white body with a gray mantle, black cap and wings, and a pointed, forked tail. The feet and bill are reddish orange. It is a graceful water bird that often hovers while searching for prey.

HABITAT AND RANGE: This bird breeds in central and eastern Canada and coastal areas of the northeastern United States. It nests on sandy beaches and feeds on marine life and large insects.

The Arctic tern (*Sterna paradisaea*) has perhaps the longest migration route of any bird. Terns from Arctic regions of the Northern Hemisphere head south in the fall and fly over the Atlantic along the coasts of England and Spain, then down past Africa to the edge of Antarctica. As they begin their journey back toward the Arctic, they retrace their spring route.

Like pelicans, terns dive head first into the water. The tern is not known for its precision and may dive a dozen or more times before coming up with a fish. One species of tern living in the tropics lays its single egg on the bare branch of a tree, balancing it perfectly on its narrow perch.

The name tern is from the Scandinavian words for "sea swallow." The family name Laridae comes from the Latin meaning "ravenous seabird." *Hirundo* is Latin for "swallow," and refers to the tern's swallow-like tail and wings.

The natural population of the least tern was threatened at the beginning of this century because the feathers were valued as decoration for women's hats. Although protective laws helped the population recover, their numbers have again dropped dramatically due to loss of habitat. Its preferred home of open, sandy beaches has been greatly reduced due to development.

BROWN THRASHER

COMMON NAME: Thrasher, Brown

SCIENTIFIC NAME: *Toxostoma rufum*

OTHER SPECIES: Sage thrasher (*Oreoscoptes montanus*)

DESCRIPTION: A slim russet-brown bird, the brown thrasher has heavy brown streaks on its lighter-colored breast. It has a long, slightly curved bill, a long tail, and two light wing bars. It is approximately 11 inches long. The sage thrasher is smaller than the brown thrasher, measuring only 8 inches. It has a gray back with white wing bars, a whitish breast with dark streaks, and white spots on the square corners of the tail.

HABITAT AND RANGE: Frequently seen in thickets, or under shrubs or brush, the brown thrasher lives in the eastern United States. The sage thrasher ranges over most of the West and South and into Mexico. Its preferred habitat is a scrub-oak forest or sagebrush in the plains. It winters in the desert.

The genus name *Toxostoma* is from the Greek for "bow-mouthed," referring to the upper mandible, which is somewhat bow-shaped. The species name *rufum* is from the Latin for "rusty red," the color of the general plumage.

The genus name for the sage thrasher, *Oreoscoptes,* is Greek for "mimic of the mountains." The bird used to be known as the mountain mockingbird.

The brown thrasher, a relative of the mockingbird, is also capable of mimicking other birds, but does not have as large a repertoire as the mockingbird. As it sings, the thrasher repeats the song phrases two or three times.

The brown thrasher became Georgia's state bird in 1970.

TUFTED TITMOUSE

COMMON NAME: Titmouse, Tufted

SCIENTIFIC NAME: *Parus bicolor*

DESCRIPTION: A quick, little, gray bird, the titmouse is only 5 inches long. It is all gray above and light gray below, with an orange blush on the sides. It has a black patch above its tiny, needle-like bill. The black-crested titmouse, in southern Texas, is similar to the tufted but has a distinct black crest.

HABITAT AND RANGE: Found in the eastern half of the United States except for northern New England and southern Florida, the titmouse is at home in many areas. Preferred habitats include mixed deciduous and coniferous forests, mesquite or scrub thickets, and suburban areas.

The common name titmouse comes from the Old Icelandic word *titr,* meaning "something small," and mouse from the Old English *mase,* meaning "small bird."

In Cherokee Indian legend, the titmouse, like the chickadee, is regarded as a messenger; unfortunately, it also has the reputation of a liar. This comes from an old legend about a wicked witch who put great fear into the people because she would eat the liver of anyone she met. The people gathered together and devised a plan to catch her. They dug a great pit and then covered it with tree limbs and leaves and moss. Then they waited for the old woman to come along and fall in. Their plan worked and the witch fell into the pit, but when they tried to kill her, their arrows could not pierce her.

Finally the little titmouse sprang up on a branch and called, "*Un, un, un*" ("Heart, heart, heart"). The people thought that the bird meant they should shoot at her heart, and they did this, but still they could not pierce the witch's tough skin. In frustration they grabbed the titmouse and, calling him a liar, cut off his tongue. This is why today the titmouse has such a short tongue.

It wasn't until the chickadee came and sat upon the witch's right hand that they were able to kill her—for her heart was found inside her hand.

RUFOUS-SIDED TOWHEE

COMMON NAME: Towhee, Rufous-sided

SCIENTIFIC NAME: *Pipilo erythrophthalmus*

DESCRIPTION: This towhee is 7 inches long and has rusty red sides, a black hood, and a long black tail with large white spots near the tip. The western variety has scattered white spots on the back and wings. The breast is white, the eye red. The female is similarly colored, though her black parts are usually more of a dusty brown.

HABITAT AND RANGE: This bird is seen throughout the United States in forests, scrubland, and on the edges of open woods. In the West it prefers open chaparral, canyons, piñon-juniper woods, and suburban areas. It eats insects, seeds, fruits, and sometimes small lizards.

The genus name *Pipilo* is from the Latin word meaning "to chirp." The species name *erythrophthalmus* is Greek for "red-eyed," denoting the red eye prominent in this species.

The name towhee was given to this bird because of its distinctive song, which sounds more nearly like "too-*whee*!" This name was given by Mark Catesby, an early English naturalist and bird artist who traveled widely in the American colonies during the years 1712–1725. The song has also been described as "Drink your tea!"

The towhee is often heard before it is seen. Like a chicken scratching for seeds, it will scratch the ground looking for grubs, insects, and seeds among the dried leaves of the forest floor. Because of the way it forages, the rufous-sided towhee has also been called the ground robin.

WILD TURKEY

COMMON NAME: Turkey, Wild
SCIENTIFIC NAME: *Meleagris gallopavo*

DESCRIPTION: The wild turkey is the largest game bird in North America. Males are 48 inches and females 36 inches in length. It has a bare, grayish head, red wattles, and a brownish iridescent body. The fanned tail of the male is erect during display. The female is similar, but smaller, and duller in coloring.

HABITAT AND RANGE: Turkeys roost in trees at night and forage on the ground for seeds, nuts, and insects during the day. They prefer mountain forests, woods, and swampy areas. Their range includes most of the United States.

Turkeys are among the oldest domestic birds in the Americas. Many of the ancient tribes of Mexico and the southwestern United States kept these birds close to their homes, fattening them up until they were needed for food.

Many native American tribes, however, considered the turkey an inferior bird—a coward—and refused to eat the meat, fearing that they, too, would become cowardly. Other tribes considered them spiritually important and actually buried them with ceremony when they died. The oldest record of such a burial was found near Flagstaff, Arizona, and dates back to A.D. 600.

Turkey feathers were often attached to a prayer stick. The feathers were given as offerings to the dead who returned to the earth for a short time before finally ascending again as clouds.

In 1511 the King of Spain requested that every Spanish ship returning home from the New World bring five male and five female turkeys with them. Within fifty years turkeys were a common sight in farmyards throughout Europe, but in the first few years after the

bird's introduction there, the word *turkey* was synonymous with anything strange or exotic.

One clan of the Pueblo Indians relates this tale about the turkey: In the early days, there came a great flood, and all the animals feared that they would drown. They said that the flood was sent to punish the tribe for their wickedness. The good people in the tribe, however, were sent turkey feathers, which allowed them to fly to the mountains to save themselves. Unused to flying, though, the members of the tribe flew too low and their tail feathers dragged in the dirty water. Turkey feathers are still stained that way today.

The Cherokee Indians tell this tale of why the turkey gobbles: All the birds and animals loved to play ball, and as they played, they liked to shout and call loudly to one another. The grouse had a fine voice in those days and was justifiably proud of it. The turkey did not have much of a voice and asked the grouse to teach him to call loudly. The grouse agreed but asked for some kind of payment, so the turkey offered some of his feathers, which the grouse still wears today as a collar around his neck. The turkey learned quickly from the grouse, until finally the day came to try out his voice. The grouse told him that he would stand up on a hollow log and when the time was right, he would signal the turkey to call as loudly as he could. All went according to plan, but when the grouse gave the signal, the turkey got so excited, all he could do was to make a gobbling sound, and that is why today, whenever the turkey hears a noise, he just gobbles.

According to Hopi mythology, the turkey was the first bird to try to raise the sun high in the sky. He was valiant in his efforts, but stayed too long near the sun. His head was burned and all the feathers came off, and he remains this way today.

The genus name *Meleagris* is Greek for "speckled" and refers to the pattern of the feathers. *Gallopavo* is from the Latin words

for "cock" and "peafowl."

American pioneers used the turkey to make many different items. The sharp spurs on the turkey's legs were made into arrowheads for hunting small game. The feathers were used as stuffing for mattresses and pillows, the wings to make brooms, and the tails as fans. Benjamin Franklin preferred the turkey over the bald eagle for our national bird, believing the turkey to be a more respectable bird and a true native of North America.

Fifty years ago the wild turkey was threatened with extinction because it was hunted so often. Government agencies have worked hard to reintroduce the turkey to various areas and to carefully manage wildlife habitats and control hunting seasons so that the turkey is once again fairly common.

COMMON NAME: **Veery**

SCIENTIFIC NAME: *Catharus fuscescens*

DESCRIPTION: Measuring a little over 6 inches in length, the veery is brown above, grayish white below. Its throat is gray, its breast a softly spotted buff color.

HABITAT AND RANGE: Veeries are spotted most frequently in wet deciduous woodlands, by streams, or along lake edges in many areas of the northern United States.

S eldom seen but often heard, the veery is a solitary bird that makes its home in the woods. It is a member of the thrush family and is more slender and lovely than most other thrushes. The song of the veery is beautiful and ephemeral, seeming to come from nowhere and then disappear, leaving only a faint echo behind. The veery begins its sweet concert at dusk.

Veeries most often feed on insects on the ground but can also catch prey such as butterflies while flying.

Catharus is Greek for "pure," which describes the song, and *fuscescens* is Latin for "dusky," referring perhaps to the hour this bird's song begins, rather than to its color, which is a brownish red.

VEERY

SOLITARY VIREO

COMMON NAME: Vireo, Solitary
SCIENTIFIC NAME: *Vireo solitarius*

DESCRIPTION: This little bird, measuring 5 inches long, is gray above, white below, and looks like it's wearing white-framed glasses. The eastern variety is yellow-olive on the back and yellow on the sides. The West Coast variety has more gray on the back, with just a hint of yellow.

HABITAT AND RANGE: These birds are found in mixed conifer and deciduous woodland areas along the West Coast, the Florida and Gulf coasts, and in the mountainous regions of the East.

Aristotle was thought to have used the name *vireo*, which is from the Latin word for "to be green," with reference to the Eurasian greenfinch. Neither the vireo nor the greenfinch, however, show much green coloration. *Solitarius* is Latin for "alone," a description of the bird's behavior, which is indeed rather hermit-like. This bird does not travel or feed in flocks and stays in the southern United States after other birds have migrated farther south.

The vireos are ground feeders, finding insects among the leaves of the forest floor. Vireos are among the best nest builders in North America. Their nests are tightly woven and are suspended from the V of forked twigs and branches.

The red-eyed vireo, *Vireo olivaceus,* is sometimes called "the preacher" on account of its long, monotonous song.

TURKEY VULTURE

COMMON NAME: Vulture, Turkey
SCIENTIFIC NAME: *Cathartes aura*

DESCRIPTION: The turkey vulture, or turkey buzzard, measures 25 to 32 inches in length, roughly the size of an eagle. It holds its long wings in a wide, shallow V. It is a black bird, with pale linings in the wings. Its tail is long, its head bare and reddish.

HABITAT AND RANGE: Turkey vultures breed in deciduous forests and woodland areas throughout the United States and winter in southern and eastern coastal states.

The name vulture is from the Latin word *vellere,* "to pluck, to tear," and refers to the feeding habits of the species. *Cathartidae,* from the Greek for "purifier" or "purger," applies to these birds because they are scavengers that "pick clean" their prey. The addition of the name turkey is justified by the bird's bare head and face, as well as its size— all similar to the turkey.

Turkey buzzards and black buzzards (*Coragyps atratus*) are both members of the family of New World vultures, a group of birds that includes the great condors of California. This group is a very ancient one, as evidenced by fossils dating back millions of years.

In the United States, a buzzard is the same thing as a vulture. In England the buzzard is considered a hawk.

The name buzzard is from an old French word, *busart,* a relative of the Latin *butes,* which refers to a broad-winged hawk. This name has been in use in England since the 1200s.

The slow-flying buzzard was never of interest to hunters, nor has it ever been considered a very important or useful bird. The word *buzzard* eventually came to mean something derogatory.

The turkey vulture was considered a harbinger of spring. Country folk believed that once this bird appeared in late winter there would be no more cold weather and it was time to plant crops.

Feathers from the black buzzard worn in the hair were thought to be an effective cure for rheumatism, and a talisman made from those feathers was thought to be protection against the scorpion's bite.

The Iroquois tell a tale that explains the vulture's baldness: In the beginning, all birds were naked but they soon became ashamed and wanted fine feathers. They were told that they could have beautiful plumage, but that someone would have to travel very far to get it. The birds chose the vulture to go and get their new clothes. The vulture, who at that time was accustomed to eating seeds and insects, like other birds, found that food was scarce on this long journey. He was forced to eat garbage and carrion, as he still does today.

When the vulture finally found the new plumage, he greedily chose the most beautiful for himself. Unfortunately, he could not fly in his new headdress and was forced to take it off—and his head has remained uncovered to this day.

A Louisiana folktale suggests that the vulture is bald today because a rabbit threw a pan full of hot ashes at his head in an act of revenge (though it is not at all clear what was being avenged).

Some Native American cultures considered the vulture a deity, the force that carried souls into the next world. In Egypt the vulture was a symbol of maternity and purification. The Nahuatl Indians, however, took it as a symbol of infirmities, misfortune, and old age. Both Aristotle and Pliny considered vultures omens of bad luck.

The vulture in ancient Egypt was revered as a symbol of the deity Nekht, whose job it was to protect the queens of Egypt. Because of this, the queens always wore headdresses that looked like vulture heads. In Persian mythology, two immense vultures guard the gates of hell.

COMMON NAME: Warbler, Yellow

SCIENTIFIC NAME: *Dendroica petechia*

DESCRIPTION: A small bird, this warbler is all yellow with rusty-red streaks on its breast. The female has very faint rufous streaks on her breast; otherwise the sexes are similar.

HABITAT AND RANGE: Yellow warblers breed in suburbia and along streams throughout the United States and Canada except in Florida and along the southern coast.

Warblers are sadly misnamed, for none of the 119 different kinds of warblers found in North America truly warble. Their songs are, instead, a combination of whispers and tweets and twitters. These birds were named by John James Audubon, probably for their similarity in behavior (rather than song) to the Old World warblers of Europe, which really do have beautiful warbling voices. Again despite its inability to sing beautifully, this bird is also called a wild canary.

The common names of some other warblers are also misleading. The Virginia warbler is not seen anywhere close to that state (having been instead named for a woman named Virginia), and the Nashville warbler is rarely seen in the country music capital, where it was first discovered in 1811.

The genus name is much more appropriate: *Dendroica* is from the Greek for "tree-dweller" and tells where these birds are most often found. The species name *petechia* is Latin for "with red spots on the skin" and is descriptive of the bird's red-streaked breast.

YELLOW WARBLER

Warblers vary from the common yellow-rumped warbler to the far less common Kirtland's warbler, which is so picky about its breeding place that it nests only in stands of young jack pines that spring up in the wake of a fire. Parts of a bird sanctuary in central Michigan are burned periodically in hopes of establishing a permanent breeding ground for this bird.

Warblers migrate at night, a habit that has proven dangerous for these birds. When they are blinded by heavy rains or high winds, they fly into skyscrapers, television towers, light-houses or other tall structures. The death toll can be startlingly high.

The cowbird often puts her eggs in the nest of the yellow warbler. The warbler sometimes rejects and sometimes accepts the foreign egg, depending on the number of her own eggs already in the nest. If she has only laid a single egg when the cowbird sneaks in hers, the warbler will probably reject both the cowbird's and her own by building another nesting layer over the eggs. If, however, the warbler has already laid two or more eggs, she will probably accept the foreign egg.

COMMON NAME: Waxwing, Cedar
SCIENTIFIC NAME: *Bombycilla cedorum*

DESCRIPTION: A brownish bird, the cedar waxwing is pale yellow below with a smooth, swept-back crest and a black band that almost encircles the crown, resembling a mask. There is a characteristic yellow band on the tip of the tail and the wings have a touch of red.

HABITAT AND RANGE: Cedar waxwings are found all across the United States and southern Canada and into Mexico. They breed in the northern half of the country and winter in the southern half. Because they enjoy berries and fruit, these birds are often found in orchards, gardens, and open woodlands.

The name waxwing refers to the small bits of red on the wings. Some people thought that they looked like spots of sealing wax. The genus name *Bombycillidae* is from Greek or Latin for "silk-tail" and refers to the yellow tip of the tail. The species earns its name *cedorum,* Latin for "of the cedars," because these birds are seen so often in the cedar tree.

Waxwings are sociable birds and have been observed to pass a berry from beak to beak until finally one hungry waxwing eats it. They can also be the most voracious eaters and will stuff themselves on berries. Some-

CEDAR WAXWING

times the berries have rotted and fermented and the birds will actually become intoxicated, resulting in a loss of coordination and control.

In Switzerland the waxwing is called *Pest-vogel* and *strebe-vogel,* meaning "pestilence bird" and "death bird." These names date back to a time when peasants would see flocks of these birds swoop into an area and strip the trees of all their berries during bitterly cold winter weather. In a confusion of cause and effect, these people believed that it was the waxwings that actually brought the cold weather and snow with them.

COMMON NAME: Whippoorwill

SCIENTIFIC NAME: *Caprimulgus vociferus*

DESCRIPTION: This bird has a large mouth, suitable for catching night-flying insects. It is a mottled gray-brown with a large flat head. The black throat is edged with a wide white band. Whippoorwills sometimes roost lengthwise on low tree branches.

HABITAT AND RANGE: Whippoorwills are usually located by their voice. They repeat their song over and over. They frequent deciduous woodlands and wooded canyons but are rarely seen during the day, as they are nocturnal and spend the daylight hours often sleeping on the forest floor, perfectly camouflaged with the dead leaves. During the day their eyes are merely a tiny slit. At night they are wide and round.

These birds are found in south-central Canada, throughout the eastern United States, and in southwestern New Mexico and southeastern Arizona.

Unmarried women used to listen carefully for the call of the whippoorwill. One call meant she wouldn't marry for at least a year. If it called three times or more, it meant she was destined to be a spinster. Two calls, the perfect number, meant impending matrimony.

The repetitious calls of the whippoorwill were often considered an omen of death. The call of this bird sounds somewhat like a question, and the Omaha Indians thought that if they answered no and the bird stopped calling immediately, the person who answered would soon die. If the bird kept calling, that person would live a long time.

WHIPPOORWILL

The Ute Indians believed that the whippoorwill was the god of the night and changed a frog into the moon by magic. The Iroquois believed that the little wildflowers known as lady's slipper were the whippoorwill's shoes.

Young whippoorwills are most often hatched when the moon is full. By coincidence (or Grand Plan) this is the time when the parent birds are best able to hunt and supply the

greatest amount of food for their offspring.

The genus name is made up of two Latin words, *caper,* meaning "goat," and *mulgere,* "to milk." It refers to a legend in which these birds attack goats and suck at their udders until they are empty and dry. Aristotle wrote of this practice and hinted that when the udders withered, the goat would go blind.

The Hopi name for this bird is "sleeping one."

COMMON NAME: Woodpecker, Downy
SCIENTIFIC NAME: *Picoides pubescens*

DESCRIPTION: This small, black and white woodpecker is about 6 inches long. It has a white back, a small bill, and a black cap with a red patch at the back of the crown. The face is black and white, the tail black, and the wings black with white markings. The female lacks the red on the crown.

HABITAT AND RANGE: Often seen on suburban shade trees, as well as in orchards and woodlands, the downy woodpecker lives throughout the lower forty-eight states, into southern Canada and Alaska.

Many Indian tribes regard the red-headed woodpecker (*Melanerpes erythrocephalus*) as sacred. The Omaha tribes consider it the protector of children because the woodpecker keeps its young in such a safe place. California Indians used the bright red feathers of the woodpecker as currency. In Christian symbolism, the woodpecker stands for heresey and Satan, although in general this bird is used as a symbol for bravery, industry, and war. A legend is told in Germany about a beautiful princess who is kept captive along

with all her fabulous wealth. The only way anyone can get to her is to carry a white woodpecker on a Friday night at midnight.

Another ancient legend suggests that the woodpecker found fire by boring into the wood. Its red head symbolizes its ability to find fire. Woodpeckers were also considered "lightning birds," creatures who could keep one safe from lightning.

There are many tales about how the woodpecker received his red head. The Algonquin Indians tell a story about two strong warriors

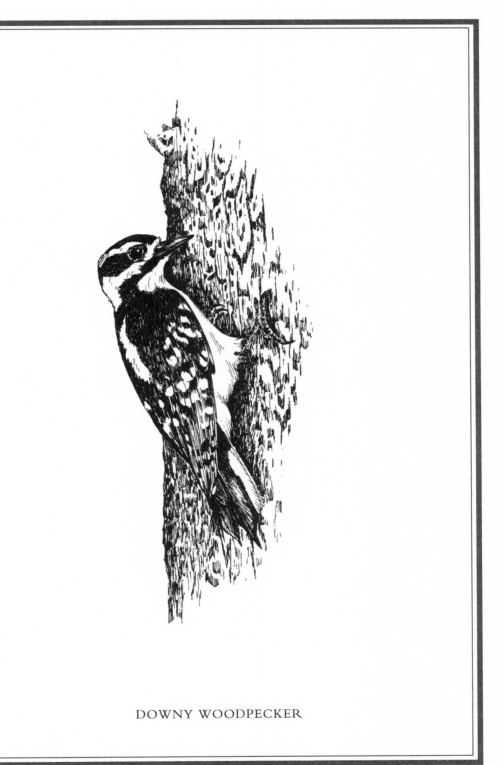

DOWNY WOODPECKER

who were fighting each other. At last one of them had only three arrows left. He had nearly given up when the woodpecker (called Ma-Ma) told him to shoot at the base of the scalp, the only place his opponent was vulnerable. The warrior did this, killing his enemy. He took the scalp from his enemy and rubbed the blood on the head of the woodpecker, who still carries this scarlet badge to this day.

The woodpecker has black at the tip of his tail because, according to the Chitimacha Indians of northern Louisiana, when the Great Flood came, the woodpecker was able to save himself by hanging onto a high tree limb by his claws. But he wasn't quite high enough and his tail dragged into the dirty water, turning it black.

Another legend tells of a woodpecker who was sitting high in a tree enjoying a piece of honeycomb. He noticed a toad sitting at the base of the tree looking at the honeycomb wistfully. The woodpecker called down, "Would you like some honeycomb?" and the toad nodded his head eagerly. With this the woodpecker lowered a small basket down for the toad and pulled him up. But just as the toad reached the honeycomb, the woodpecker let go of the basket and the toad landed with a thud on the ground. The little toad was furious at this trickery and began to drink. Soon he had drunk up all the rivers and lakes in the country and there was a severe drought everywhere. The little toad was so happy at his revenge that he began to dance and as he danced, water began to pour out of his body until finally the drought was over. *Pubescens,* the species name, is from the Latin word meaning "coming into puberty" or "showing the first signs of beard," a reference to the woodpecker's soft, fluffy feathers.

The bill is used primarily to gather food but is also used to tap out a territorial signal to rivals. Woodpeckers have special "shock absorbers" in their heads that allow them to drill holes into hard greenwood. All woodpeckers have strong claws, short legs, and stiff tail feathers, enabling them to climb tree trunks with ease.

COMMON NAME: Woodcock, American
SCIENTIFIC NAME: *Scolopax minor*

DESCRIPTION: A chubby bird nearly 10 inches long, the American woodcock has a long bill, a short neck, and short legs. This nocturnal bird is mottled black, brown, and gray. The underparts are tan, with a hint of rose. The back of the head is black with two tan bars, and a rosy tan tail shows a wide black band.

HABITAT AND RANGE: Seen throughout eastern Canada and the United States east of the Mississippi River, woodcocks prefer moist woodland areas.

AMERICAN WOODCOCK

Woodcocks feed almost exclusively on earthworms, which they locate with their sensitive probing bill. The eyes of this bird are situated far up on its head so that it can keep a lookout for danger even while probing the ground; and because it often feeds in dim light, its eyes are very large. The woodcock sometimes thumps its feet against the ground, presumably to startle worms into motion.

Other common names for this species include bogsucker, timberdoodle, hookumpake, and night peck.

COMMON NAME: Wood Thrush

SCIENTIFIC NAME: *Hylocichla mustelina*

DESCRIPTION: Slightly rotund, the wood thrush is about 8 inches long, rufous-brown above its white breast with dark spots.

HABITAT AND RANGE: This bird prefers moist, deciduous forest; in the absence of that it will settle for mixed woods, swamps, or suburbia. Its range encompasses the eastern United States, except for the Florida peninsula. It is sometimes found in the West and is slowly extending its range into Canada.

The name thrush is used to identify such well-known favorites as robins, bluebirds, chats, redstarts, and nightingales. Thirteen species of thrushes breed in the United States.

The thrushes' songs are known for their beauty—especially that of the nightingale. The white-rumped shama of Indian is a thrush with such a beautiful song that it is often kept as a caged bird.

The following Greek myth is told about the swallow and the nightingale: King Tereus of Thrace married the beautiful Procne, but when he met her sister, Philomela, he fell violently in love with her. The king raped his sister-in-law, and then, in terror that his crime would be discovered, cut out her tongue so that she could not tell. The gods, taking pity on Philomela, turned her into a nightingale, and her sister into a swallow. That is why the swallow only chatters but the nightingale mourns.

The hermit thrush, *Catharus guttatus,* is the state bird of Vermont, where it is particularly beloved for its beautiful song. The naturalist John Burroughs wrote of the call of the hermit thrush: "Listening to this strain on the lone mountain, with the full moon just rounded on the horizon, the pomp of your

WOOD THRUSH

cities and the pride of your civilization seemed trivial and cheap."

In Ireland, an unknown poet wrote: ". . . the carol of the thrush, pleasant and familiar above my house."

The wood thrush, which eats such pests as cutworms, beetles, and snails, is welcomed by gardeners.

COMMON NAME: Wren, House

SCIENTIFIC NAME: *Troglodytes aedon*

DESCRIPTION: The little wren, 5 inches long, is brown above and a creamy buff below. Its bill is small and slightly decurved. It has a faint, buff eye-ring and barred wings.

HABITAT AND RANGE: House wrens frequent scattered woodlands, suburban areas, and gardens throughout the United States and southern Canada; they winter in southern coastal areas.

The wren figures prominently in folklore worldwide. A story is told in many different cultures about the birds trying to choose a king by seeing who could fly the highest. The wren almost always wins, usually by outwitting the eagle in various ways. In most of the stories, the wren wins by riding on the eagle's back, thus being the highest. A slight variation of this is told in which the wren hides under the eagle's wing rather than on its back or tail and then flies up just before the contest ends. In some versions of the story, the eagle is so enraged at the wren's trickery that he attacks the wren, removing part of its tail, so that thereafter the little bird has to fly low.

Other variants of this story tell of the title going to whoever can fly the *lowest*. Again,

the wren wins through his cleverness; he flies down a mouse hole.

Wrens generally lay many eggs. A country verse pays tribute to the powers of the wren:

Coo-oo Coo-oo
It's as much as a pigeon can do
To maintain two,
But the little wren can maintain ten
And bring them all up like gentlemen.

The poet James Russell Lowell wrote of a pair of wrens: "He sings to the wide world and she to her nest, / In the nice ear of Nature, which song is best?"

The wren has always figured prominently not only in verse and song but also in ceremony and superstition. The Wren Hunt is a

HOUSE WREN

medieval tradition that is carried out in various forms in many European countries. Customarily, wrens are hunted (or in some cases decorated) on Saint Stephen's Day (December 26). The story behind this practice is that a bird awakened Saint Stephen's guards as he was escaping. Another explanation as to the origin of the hunt holds that as the Irish army was preparing a surprise attack, a wren hopped on a drum and awakened the Danes, who jumped up and defended themselves.

The wren hunt was purely ceremonial, and the killing of the wren was sacrificial. The bird itself, which was killed only at this one time of year, was buried with ceremony, and the feathers were considered talismans.

Even in the midst of a Wren Hunt, it was often easier to talk about catching wrens than it was to actually get your hands on one of these little birds, as evidenced by a song written by the poet Waterford:

We were all day hunting the wren;
We were all day hunting the wren;
The wren so cute and cunning,
He stayed in the bush when we were
running.

Aristotle wrote of this bird: "The wren inhabits shrubberies and holes and cannot easily be caught. Now it is shy and of a feeble habit, but endowed with great ability of getting food and knowledge of its craft."

In Ireland, where the wren was referred to as *"magus avium"* ("greatest of birds"), it was thought to be able to tell the future, and records predicting future events based on the wren's behavior have existed for hundreds of years there.

The name wren is the modern form of the Middle and Old English word for "lascivious." It is not clear why this bird was given this name. The genus name *Troglodytes* is from the Greek for "cave dweller," after the mythical cave-dwelling people of Ethiopia. It is thought to suggest the wren's constant seeking for cover. The species name *aedon* is Greek for "songstress." The myth of Aedon, who kills her own son by mistake, is actually associated with the nightingale. Some people believe that the wren sounds like the nightingale and for that reason was given this name.

A nice twist to an old proverb is: "Better a wren in the hand than a crane on the wing."

In *Richard III,* Shakespeare writes: ". . . wrens make prey where eagles dare not perch."

The little cactus wren, which makes its home in the giant saguaro cactus, is the state bird of Arizona.

COMMON NAME: Yellowthroat, Common

SCIENTIFIC NAME: *Geothlypis trichas*

DESCRIPTION: This little bird measures only 4 1/2 to 6 inches in length and has a black mask, yellow throat and breast, and a white belly. The wings, tail, and back are dark olive.

HABITAT AND RANGE: Found most frequently in cattail bogs, marshes, and wet, brushy areas, the yellowthroat breeds in most of Canada, except for the Northwest Territory, and throughout the United States.

The genus name *Geothlypis* is from the Greek for "earth bird" and presumably was assigned to this bird because it ate seeds and berries close to the earth. Research has determined, however, that this bird eats more insects than seeds.

Its song is clear and bubbly, sounding like "witchy-witchy-witchy."

The males of this species have a distinctive black "bandit" mask. When, in an experiment, a similar-looking mask was taped to a stuffed yellowthroat female, the male mistook the stuffed bird for another male and attacked it ferociously.

Although the yellowthroat is quite common, it is rarely seen; more often its song is heard. The Reader's Digest *Book of North American Birds* suggests that the squeaking noise made by kissing the back of one's hand will sometimes draw these curious birds into view.

COMMON YELLOWTHROAT

SELECTED BIBLIOGRAPHY

Audubon Society. *Field Guide to North American Birds,* Eastern Region. New York: Alfred A. Knopf, 1977.

Austin, Elizabeth and Oliver L. Austin, Jr. *The Random House Book of Birds.* New York: Random House, 1970.

Betty, John. *Hummingbirds.* Chicago: Follett, 1960.

Bulfinch, Thomas. *Bulfinch's Mythology: The Age of Fable, The Age of Chivalry: Legends of Charlemagne.* The Modern Library Publisher, n.d.

Campbell, Joseph. *The Way of the Animal Powers.* New York: Harper and Row, 1983.

Cassidy, James, editor. *Book of North American Birds.* Pleasantville, N.Y.: Reader's Digest Books, 1990.

Cavendish, Richard. *Illustrated Encyclopedia of Mythology, Religion, and the Unknown.* New York: Marshall Cavendish, 1983.

Flegg, Jim. *Birdlife.* New York: Pelham, 1986.

Halle, Louis Joseph. *The Storm Petrel and the Owl of Athena.* Princeton, N.J.: Princeton University Press, 1970.

Hume, Rob. *A Birdwatcher's Miscellany.* London: Blandford Press, 1984.

Ingersoll, Ernest. *Birds in Legend, Fable and Folklore.* London: Longmans, Green and Co., 1923.

Jewkes, W. T. *Man the Myth Maker.* New York: Harcourt Brace Javanovich, 1981.

Jobes, Gertrude. *Dictionary of Mythology, Folklore and Symbols.* Metuchen, N.J.: Scarecrow Press, Inc., 1962.

Krutch, Joseph Wood. *A Treasury of Birdlore.* New York: Doubleday, 1962.

Leach, Maria, editor. *Funk & Wangalls' Standard Dictionary of Folklore.* Mahwah, N.J.: Funk & Wagnalls, 1972.

Limburg, Peter R. *What's In The Names of Birds.* Coward McCann and Geooheoan, 1975.

Mercatante, Anthony. *Zoo of the Gods.* New York: Harper and Row, 1974.

Peattie, Donald Culross. *A Cup of Sky.* Boston: Houghton Mifflin Company, 1950.

Singer, Arthur and Alan Singer. *State Birds.* New York: Lodestar Books, 1986.

Stefferud, Alfred, editor. *Birds in our Lives.* New York: Arco Publishing Co., 1970.

Sutton, Ann and Myron Sutton. *Eastern Forests.* New York: Chanticleer Press, 1985.

Weidensaul, Scott. *The Birder's Miscellany: a fascinating collection of facts.* New York: Simon and Schuster, 1991.

Wernert, Susan J., editor. *North American Wildlife.* Pleasantville, N.Y.: Reader's Digest Books, 1986.

INDEX

Enjoying Nature

Here are some other fine titles on nature and the environment. All Globe Pequot nature titles are written by experts in their fields and cover many aspects of nature, from identifying flora and fauna to conserving the environment. Please check your local bookstore for other fine Globe Pequot Press titles, which include:

The Folklore of Trees and Shrubs, $24.95

Wildflower Folklore, $23.95

Wildflower Folklore (paper), $14.95

Garden Flower Folklore, $19.95

The Wildflower Meadow Book, $16.95

Good Dirt, $19.95 HC

Animals in the Family, $11.95

Birding for the Amateur Naturalist, $8.95

River Reflections, $13.95

The Frail Ocean, $14.95

Private Lives of Garden Birds, $12.95

The World of Birds, $15.95

Where the Whales Are, $12.95

Where the Animals Are, $12.95

The Nocturnal Naturalist, $17.95 HC

Botany for All Ages, $12.95

Wild Mammals of New England, $9.95

A Guide to the New England Landscape, $9.95

Marine Wildlife of Puget Sound, $12.95

Wild Edible Plants, $9.95

Birdwatching For All Ages, $13.95

To order any of these titles with MasterCard or Visa, call toll-free, (800) 243–0495; in Connecticut call (800) 962–0973. Free shipping for orders of three or more books. Shipping charge of $3.00 per book for one or two books ordered. Connecticut residents add sales tax. Ask for your free catalogue of Globe Pequot's quality books on recreation, travel, nature, gardening, cooking, crafts, and more. Prices and availability subject to change.